SOLO Taxonom
A Guide for Schools

Planning for differentiation   **Book 2**

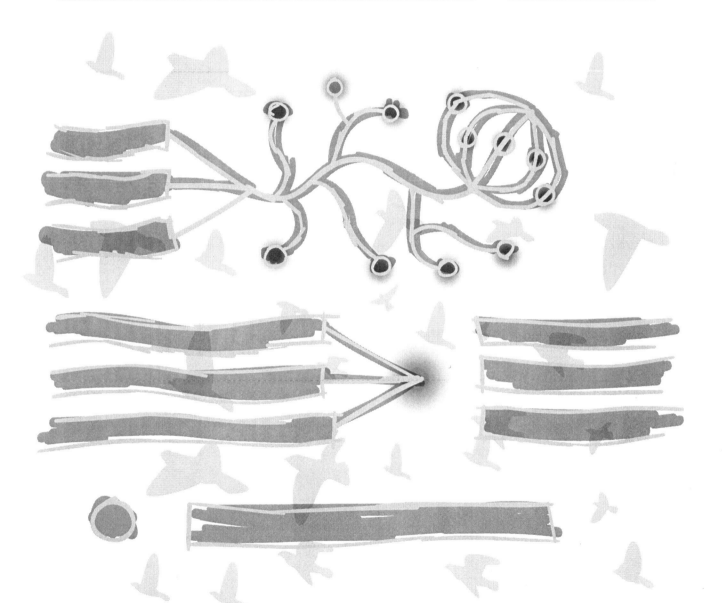

Pam Hook and Julie Mills

essential
resources

Title: SOLO Taxonomy: A Guide for Schools
Book 2: Planning for differentiation

Authors: Pam Hook and Julie Mills

Editor: Tanya Tremewan

Designer: Freshfields Graphic Design

Book code: 5638

ISBN: 978-1-927143-96-4

Published: 2012

Publisher: Essential Resources Educational Publishers Limited

United Kingdom:	**Australia:**	**New Zealand:**
Units 8–10 Parkside	PO Box 906	PO Box 5036
Shortgate Lane	Strawberry Hills	Invercargill
Laughton BN8 6DG	NSW 2012	
ph: 0845 3636 147	ph: 1800 005 068	ph: 0800 087 376
fax: 0845 3636 148	fax: 1800 981 213	fax: 0800 937 825

Websites: www.essentialresourcesuk.com
www.essentialresources.com.au
www.essentialresources.co.nz

Copyright: Text: © Pam Hook and Julie Mills, 2012
Edition and illustrations:
© Essential Resources Educational Publishers Limited, 2012

About the authors: Pam Hook is an educational consultant (HookED www.pamhook.com), who works with New Zealand schools to develop curricula and pedagogies for learning to learn based on SOLO Taxonomy. She has published articles on thinking, learning, e-learning and gifted education, writes curriculum material for government and business, directs Ministry of Education e-learning contracts and is co-author of two science textbooks widely used in New Zealand secondary schools. She is known for her educational blog (http://artichoke.typepad.com) and is a popular keynote speaker at conferences.

Julie Mills has been an educational consultant in learning and teaching since 2005, working in schools throughout New Zealand with a focus on raising student achievement. With a depth of understanding of curriculum, achievement and assessment practices, she facilitates a range of contracts for the Ministry of Education and writes educational resources for both the public and private sectors. She presents regularly at conferences as well as working closely with principals who are initiating change in schools. Julie has an extensive background in teaching at all primary and intermediate levels. She has also held senior management positions and was a founding school principal for four years.

Contents

Introduction

SOLO Taxonomy: A Guide for Schools is a series designed to help teachers and schools implement a common understanding and language of learning that will help students "learn to learn". At its heart is SOLO Taxonomy, a model developed by John Biggs and Kevin Collis which has proven its value to teachers and students at all primary and secondary levels. Guided by this series you can realise the many benefits of SOLO Taxonomy, such as its capacity to make learning outcomes visible, identify their level of cognitive complexity, and consequently make feedback and "feed forward" more effective in the learning process.

A focus of this second book in the series is to help teachers, principals and students to harness SOLO Taxonomy to use a common language of learning, and in particular to plan learning experiences to:

- ensure *cognitive stretch* for all students
- build *interest* for all students
- enhance the *confidence* of all students
- enable *power sharing* for all students
- integrate *information and communication technology (ICT)* into differentiated learning environments.

A second major focus is to help students self assess their learning outcomes against each learning intention, and use three-level assessment for learning tasks and the knowledge producing research process.

The five sections take you through the Hooked-on-Thinking SOLO Differentiated Curriculum Model (HOT SOLO DCM), an effective process for differentiated planning and design for learning:

1. **Essential components of the HOT SOLO DCM** outlines the purpose, challenge and solutions of the model.

2. **Implementing the HOT SOLO DCM approach** sets out ideas and templates for planning differentiated learning goals, developing differentiated success criteria, differentiating learning interventions (ICT resources and thinking skills and strategies), checking for relevance and authenticity and meeting the principles of the New Zealand Curriculum.

3. **HOT SOLO DCM sample plan** provides an exemplar for using the HOT SOLO DCM with achievement objectives from the New Zealand Curriculum.

4. **Conclusions** wraps up the gains in achievement, interest and confidence that result when students learn with experiences designed using the HOT SOLO DCM.

5. **Where to next?** introduces the key competencies and e-competencies for living well and learning well with others as the important next step in the learning process with SOLO Taxonomy.

At the back of the book is an index of all of the templates and tables set out in the book.

Please note

The website addresses (URLs) given in this book are correct at the time of publication. However, website addresses can change, and some websites may adopt advertising that is inappropriate for the classroom. It is therefore advisable to check each website you plan to use in the classroom before actually using it with your students. Essential Resources takes no responsibility for the content of any website included in this book.

1. Essential components of the HOT SOLO DCM

In this section we introduce the fundamentals of the Hooked-on-Thinking SOLO Differentiated Curriculum Model (HOT SOLO DCM), focusing on:

- its purpose
- the challenges it must address
- the solutions that it offers through SOLO Taxonomy.

Purpose

What do diverse students living in a changing world need to learn? Identifying and responding to the learning needs of a wide range of students (living in local communities in a rapidly changing world) is challenging because a purposeful curriculum must focus on maintaining the relevance of both the knowledge-building potential and the domain expertise of all students into the future (Hook, in press).

The HOT SOLO DCM is a curriculum model that offers this form of "future proofing". It respects individual abilities and interests, encourages the student to identify and assess their own learning needs (with support from the institution) and connects students with their local community.

The HOT SOLO DCM focuses on

- "teaching for understanding" rather than "teaching for knowing" (Wiske 1998)
- making learning outcomes visible through SOLO Taxonomy (Biggs and Collis 1982)
- producing knowledge by identifying local and community needs (Bigum 2004).

The pedagogical design integrates:

- "learning to learn"
- knowledge building for identified local and community needs
- differentiated student learning outcomes (SOLO constructive alignment)
- self assessment of learning outcomes (HOT SOLO rubrics)
- teacher and/or student implementation
- alignment with a concept curriculum and/or the New Zealand Curriculum.

When students plan for (and assess) their learning they "learn to learn" and take active, skilled roles in knowledge building. The HOT SOLO DCM is designed for flexible provision where content, process, product and learning environment are supported by the educational system but can be determined (and led) by the individual learner. When we place the learner at the centre of teaching and learning in the HOT SOLO DCM, we align the curriculum with the New Zealand Curriculum vision of "young people who will be confident, connected, actively involved, lifelong learners" (Ministry of Education 2007, p 7).

Our experience with schools across New Zealand shows teachers and students easily translate the HOT SOLO DCM into practical learning programmes (developed online and offline) in which SOLO-differentiated learning intentions (learning goals), students' learning experiences and self assessment of student learning outcomes are clearly aligned.

Challenges

A pedagogical design framework that enhances the learning, interest and confidence of diverse students in inclusive classrooms must provide practical solutions to the following challenges:

- How can I design responsive learning environments in inclusive classrooms that:
  - ensure cognitive stretch for all students
  - build interest for all students
  - build the confidence of all students
  - share power among all students
  - effectively integrate ICT into differentiated learning environments?
- How can I evaluate the effectiveness of these design frameworks in terms of their ability to enhance student learning outcomes, interest and confidence?

Underlying these challenges is the need for qualitative differentiation, which is "best practice" for meeting the learning needs of diverse students, including those who are gifted and talented (Ministry of Education 2000, p 36). It forms an essential part of the design planning for responsive learning environments that provide cognitive stretch for all students. However, it remains a challenge for schools to implement and sustain differentiation of curriculum, pedagogy or learning environment that is both effective and widespread.

To differentiate learning experiences qualitatively, teachers must assess the individual learning needs of all students, and design learning experiences to accommodate the learning differences and individual needs identified. Teachers may respond in various ways to such a prospect. Some are "overwhelmed by the expectation that they must qualitatively differentiate the learning experiences of every student they teach" (Hook 2006). In strictly timetabled secondary schools, for example, where classes change on the hour, this task would mean an individual teacher would need to differentiate the learning experiences of over 150 students each day.

Other teachers remain undaunted and are determined to find ways to differentiate learning experiences for their students. Yet they are often disappointed by the lack of practical advice on the "how to" of differentiation (Hook, in press). Although they may have a "checkbox audit" (Taylor 2001), bullet-pointed "should be exhortations" for differentiating content, process and product (Riley et al 2004, p 33), or "fill in the gap", core and complex, differentiated planning templates based on Bloom's taxonomy (Roberts & Roberts 2001), such resources are challenging to implement in inclusive learning environments (Hook 2006).

Solutions

The HOT SOLO DCM offers solutions to the challenges identified above, in particular through its basis in SOLO Taxonomy and its promotion of knowledge-producing schools.

SOLO Taxonomy

SOLO Taxonomy is a solution to the challenge of planning for differentiation. As a model of learning outcomes, it provides a simple and robust way of describing how learning outcomes grow in complexity from surface to deep to conceptual understanding (Biggs and Collis 1982). As it is content independent, it is useful as a generic measure of understanding across different disciplines. It provides explicit criteria for assessing the different levels of cognitive complexity of students' declarative and functioning understanding when mastering any new learning.

SOLO describes the five levels of student understanding when encountering new learning (see Table 1). The distinction between each level is clearly categorised; teachers and students tend to agree on the SOLO level of a learning outcome.

Table 1: Levels of understanding in SOLO Taxonomy

   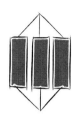 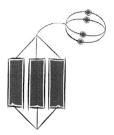

Prestructural	Unistructural	Multistructural	Relational	Extended abstract
Learning outcomes show unconnected information, with no organisation.	Learning outcomes show simple connections but importance of different parts is not noted.	Learning outcomes show connections are made, but significance of parts to overall meaning is missing.	Learning outcomes show full connections are made, and synthesis of parts to the overall meaning.	Learning outcomes go beyond subject and links are made to other concepts – generalisations.

At the **prestructural level** of understanding (**Whakarangaranga**), the student attacks the task inappropriately, having missed the point, or needs help to start.

 For example: *"I need help to define sustainability."*

The next two levels, unistructural and multistructural, are associated with bringing in information. At the **unistructural level** (**Rangaranga Takitahi**), one aspect of the task is picked up, and student understanding is disconnected and limited.

 For example: *"My definition statement has one relevant idea about sustainability."*
Unistructural response: *"Sustainability is about making sure what we do will help us live well."*

The jump to the **multistructural level** (**Rangaranga Maha**) is quantitative. Here several aspects of the task are known but their relationships to each other and the whole are missed.

 For example: *"My definition statement has several relevant ideas about sustainability."*
Multistructural response: *"Sustainability is about making sure what we do will help us live well, now and in the future. It involves long-term management of the resources for living well – for example, environmental resources, social resources and economic resources."*

The progression to relational and extended abstract outcomes is qualitative. At the **relational level** (**Whanaungatanga**), the aspects are linked and integrated, and contribute to a coherent understanding of the whole.

 For example: *"My definition statement has several relevant ideas about sustainability, and links these in some way."*
Relational response: *"Sustainability is about making sure what we do will help us live well, now and in the future. It involves long-term management of the resources for living well – for example, environmental resources, social resources and economic resources. This management is necessary **because** many of the resources we use today come from the past or from over-exploiting present resources and will not be available in the future."*

At the **extended abstract level** (**Waitara Whānui**), the student re-thinks their new relational-level understanding at another level, looks at it in a new way, and uses it as the basis for prediction, generalisation, reflection or creation of new understanding.

For example: *"My definition statement has several relevant ideas about sustainability, links these and looks at these linked ideas in a new way."*

Extended abstract response: *"Sustainability is about making sure what we do will help us live well, now and in the future. It involves long-term management of the resources for living well – for example, environmental resources, social resources and economic resources. This management is necessary because many of the resources we use today come from the past or from over-exploiting present resources and will not be available in the future.* **In my opinion** *we need to reconnect people with other people and with the natural world because it will help them to value what we have and want to protect it for future generations by managing their consumption."*

Knowledge-producing schools

We achieve relevant and authentic learning when learning goals are designed in contexts that enable knowledge production – a research process whereby diverse students "produce knowledge for [the] local community and in doing so develop new and productive community partnerships" (Bigum 2004, p 53).

Sharing power in differentiated learning environments turns teachers into researchers and investigators alongside students. When designing for power sharing, teachers must consider their students' "concerns, questions, and prior knowledge", which may lead them to give up some of their own ideas (Fraser 2000, p 35).

In schools using the HOT SOLO DCM for *power sharing* and *knowledge production*, students are researchers and creators of local knowledge through the adoption of constructivist pedagogies. When Hawera Primary students collaborated to explore the natural features of Taranaki, for example, they were intent on building new community knowledge to include in a safe travel resource for visitors to the area. The senior classes (Years 4 to 6) each focused on one area: rivers and dams; gas and oil fields; Mount Taranaki; or beaches and coastline. Classes became experts on one of these built or natural resources, sharing their findings with the wider group. They then headed off for a two-day geological adventure using their unique perspective as young travellers to look at safe travel aspects along the way. Students visited the Patea Museum where the education outside the classroom (EOTC) officer shared a programme on rivers and dams. After an overnight camp in the school hall, they went around the mountain, taking in Kupe gas field, coastline, beaches, lahars and Puke Ariki Museum. They had an opportunity to climb the mountain and take part in a bush walk before they returned to school to build useful knowledge for their community – a safe travel resource guide for youthful geological adventurers in the Taranaki area.

This SOLO planned inquiry, developed through a New Zealand Transport Agency curriculum resource, encouraged students to think like road safety planners and like geological adventurers. The process "gave a clear pathway for students and led to surprise outcomes as children raised their own questions and did additional research" (New Zealand Transport Agency 2011). Consequently students produced new knowledge of value to their community.

2. Implementing the HOT SOLO DCM approach

The HOT SOLO DCM provides an innovative approach to differentiation. It achieves this by:

- actively involving students in designing and assessing their own learning
- using SOLO Taxonomy to differentiate content, process and product (Hook in press).

When teachers (and students) use the HOT SOLO DCM to plan differentiated learning outcomes that provide explicit, proximate and explicit cognitive challenge for all students, they answer the challenges of differentiation and raise everyone's achievement outcomes and assessment capability. This approach enables *power sharing* and enhances students' interest in and confidence with the learning activities.

The sheer simplicity of SOLO Taxonomy as a model of learning means both teachers and students can use it to differentiate learning intentions, success criteria and learning experiences at different levels of cognitive complexity. Students can use SOLO-differentiated success criteria to assess the cognitive complexity of their own learning outcomes. This information then helps to identify the "where to next?" steps in learning, particularly in relation to determining future learning needs, differentiating new learning goals and identifying effective learning interventions and strategies. Our experience is that the skilled and active involvement of students throughout the differentiation process helps raise their levels of achievement, interest and confidence.

When they understand differentiation through SOLO Taxonomy, students and teachers can design learning goals that challenge but are achievable. One result can be a call for power sharing. If we use SOLO to make learning intentions, learning experiences and assessment visible, we open the way for students to be actively and skilfully involved in designing, experiencing and assessing their own learning. For example, students can plan their own learning experiences to:

- build relevant and authentic knowledge for their local community using constructive alignment
- use HOT SOLO visual maps and ICT as effective strategies
- use SOLO self assessment rubrics as success criteria and for "where to next?" steps when building knowledge.

It can be challenging to support students' "concerns, questions, and prior knowledge" when producing knowledge for local communities through self-directed, collaborative research. Students need help to, for example:

- think like a road safety planner when researching access to geological features in their local community
- survey local commuters like a tour guide operator when investigating transport options
- broadcast like a journalist when reporting on a local event
- consult like a community worker when discovering how new students could be helped to settle in school
- design experiments like an environmental scientist when mapping a local waterway (Hook, in press).

Producing knowledge with differentiated goals in the HOT SOLO DCM framework provides a practical response to the principles in the New Zealand Curriculum (NZC). The approach places the learner at the centre of teaching and learning, and in the design for learning it makes explicit: high expectations, the Treaty of Waitangi, cultural diversity, inclusion, learning to learn, community engagement, coherence and future focus.

When the educational system supports content, process, product and learning environment but the individual learner can determine (and lead) them, students have freedom and control over their own learning, and as a result their levels of achievement, interest and confidence are enhanced.

Template I gives an overview of the HOT SOLO Differentiated Curriculum Planner, which can be used to anchor the HOT SOLO DCM framework. The subsections that follow look more specifically at how to implement the approach in terms of:

- differentiating learning goals
- differentiating success criteria
- differentiating learning interventions
- checking learning goals are relevant and authentic
- meeting NZC principles.

Numerous templates are included to support the implementation of the HOT SOLO DCM.

Differentiating learning goals

SOLO Taxonomy (Biggs and Collis 1982) helps raise achievement, interest and confidence by making differentiated learning outcomes visible to students. Students "learn to learn" with a common language of SOLO learning verbs they (and their teachers) can use when designing differentiated learning experiences for a learning goal (a process known as *constructive alignment*).

The HOT SOLO maps and self assessment rubrics for the SOLO learning verbs provide effective strategies and differentiated success criteria for each differentiated goal or learning intention.

Because of this differentiation of both learning intention and success criteria, students have explicit answers for three self-regulation questions:

1. **Where am I going?** (Be explicit about the learning task.) What is my task? What are my goals? What is my learning intention (SOLO-coded)? What are my success criteria (SOLO-differentiated)?

2. **How am I going?** (Self assess progress against success criteria.) How does my learning outcome meet the success criteria (SOLO-differentiated) for the task?

3. **Where to next?** (Set next learning steps based on "Where I am going?" and "How I am going?") What new goals (SOLO-coded) can I set for myself?

Designing relevant learning intentions using SOLO and the process of constructive alignment focuses on understanding goals (concepts, NZC achievement objective or achievement standard) in ways that engage and challenge students. Constructive alignment uses SOLO learning verbs to clarify the specific learning intentions to support student understanding. In making learning intentions (and thus learning experiences and assessment) visible to students, SOLO ensures *power sharing* and *cognitive stretch* for all.

Any learning goal can be unpacked using SOLO learning verbs in the process of constructive alignment. Table 2 shows how a concept, an achievement objective and an achievement standard can be broken down into achievable learning intentions (explicit, proximate and hierarchical) using SOLO learning verbs. Each of these verbs is accompanied by a HOT visual process map and a rubric with SOLO-coded success criteria (see the next section).

Teachers (and students) can select learning intentions from the list set out in the HOT SOLO Differentiated Curriculum Planner (see Template I) and plan learning experiences to meet the identified learning intentions.

When we use SOLO verbs to unpack the concept, achievement objective or achievement standard, we can be sure that the learning intentions address the learning needs of diverse students and scaffold for deep learning outcomes. The learning process in the learning intention is explicit when each SOLO learning verb has a HOT SOLO map and differentiated self assessment rubric.

planning format

Template 1: HOT SOLO Differentiated Curriculum Planner

Concept	Context	Values	Key competencies	Key understanding	Driving question	Subsidiary questions/tasks*
	Local National Global	Excellence Innovation Diversity Equity Community and participation Ecological sustainability Integrity Respect	Thinking Managing self Participating and contributing Relating to others Making meaning from language, symbols and text			1. Multistructural outcome 2. Relational outcome 3. Extended abstract outcome

Curriculum learning area		Achievement objectives	Curriculum level: ____	Learning intentions	
Select the learning area and essence statement that best match the concept and context for your students.		Select the achievement objectives that best match the abilities of your students.		Develop using constructive alignment and SOLO learning verbs: *define, describe, sequence, classify, compare and contrast, explain, form an analogy, analyse, generalise, predict, evaluate, create.* Use these learning intentions to write your "We are learning to" statements.	

Learning experiences

Identify the learning experiences that best meet the learning intentions and achievement objectives that match your students' abilities.

Multistructural: Bringing in ideas	Relational: Linking ideas	Extended abstract: Putting linked ideas in another context
(identify, label, list, define, describe, retell, recall, recite)	*(sequence, classify, compare and contrast, identify cause and effect, analyse part–whole, explain, form an analogy, question)*	*(predict, hypothesise, generalise, imagine, reflect, evaluate, create)*

* For assessing understanding of concept, achievement objective, assessment standard or intended learning outcome.

continued ...

Thinking interventions that target bringing in ideas

(Select thinking resources and strategies to support multistructural learning experiences.)

e-learning interventions to enhance conditions for bringing in ideas

(Select ICT resources and strategies to support multistructural learning experiences.)

Thinking interventions that target linking ideas

(Select thinking resources and strategies to support relational learning experiences.)

e-learning interventions to enhance conditions for linking ideas

(Select ICT resources and strategies to support relational learning experiences.)

Thinking interventions that target putting linked ideas in another context

(Select thinking resources and strategies to support extended abstract learning experiences.)

e-learning interventions to enhance conditions for putting linked ideas in another context

(Select ICT resources and strategies to support extended abstract learning experiences.)

Self assessment rubrics for subsidiary questions/tasks

Multistructural learning outcome

Extended abstract	
Relational	
Multistructural	
Unistructural	
Prestructural	

Relational learning outcome

Extended abstract	
Relational	
Multistructural	
Unistructural	
Prestructural	

Extended abstract learning outcome

Extended abstract	
Relational	
Multistructural	
Unistructural	
Prestructural	

Teaching resources

(Identify resources to support bringing in ideas, connecting ideas, and putting ideas into another context.)

"What if" questions

(Create these for class/group discussion or writing.)

Integration

(Identify ways to integrate learning with other learning areas.)

Table 2: Constructive alignment using learning verbs from HOT SOLO maps

Constructive alignment of a learning target using HOT SOLO verbs What can be …	Concept	Achievement objective	Achievement standard
Example	Change	Social Sciences: Level 2 Understand how time and change affect people's lives	Social Studies 1.1 Describe how cultures change.
defined	Define change.	Define change in people's lives.	Define culture. Define change.
described	Describe a change.	Describe a change in people's lives. Describe a time in people's lives.	Describe a culture before, during and after change.
sequenced	Sequence a change.	Sequence a change in people's lives. Sequence a timeline in people's lives.	Sequence the changes in a culture over time.
classified	Classify changes.	Classify changes in people's lives. Classify times in people's lives.	Classify cultures. Classify changes that occur in cultures.
compared and contrasted	Compare and contrast changes.	Compare and contrast changes in people's lives. Compare and contrast times in people's lives.	Compare and contrast cultures. Compare and contrast cultural changes.
explained (causes)	Explain the causes of a change.	Explain the causes of a change in people's lives. Explain the causes of a time in people's lives.	Explain the causes of a change in a culture.
explained (effects)	Explain the effects of a change.	Explain the effects of a change in people's lives. Explain the effects of a time in people's lives.	Explain the effects of a change in a culture.
formed as an analogy	Form an analogy about a change.	Form an analogy about a change in people's lives. Form an analogy about a time in people's lives	Form an analogy about cultural change.
generalised	Generalise about change.	Generalise about a change in people's lives. Generalise about a time in people's lives.	Generalise about cultural change.
predicted	Predict a change.	Make a prediction about a change in people's lives. Make a prediction about a time in people's lives.	Make a prediction about cultural change.
evaluated	Evaluate a change.	Evaluate a change in people's lives. Evaluate a time in people's lives.	Evaluate cultural change.
created	Create a change.	Create a proposal for a change in people's lives.	Create a model for cultural change.

Furthermore, through constructive alignment the HOT SOLO DCM meets the NZC principles of *inclusion* and *high expectations* because it creates a framework of differentiated learning intentions to address all students' learning needs. Constructive alignment develops proximate and hierarchical learning intentions so that all students:

- experience challenge
- are encouraged to achieve personal excellence through a careful scaffold of steps.

Introducing a common language of learning through the SOLO verbs and HOT SOLO maps helps to implement the NZC principle of *learning to learn*. When students know themselves as "learners", they are also more likely to experience *engagement while learning*.

Finally, when we keep the goal focused on the NZC learning areas, essence statements and achievement objective (and achievement standard), the learning experiences align to the disciplinary knowledge and skills needed to build coherent understanding of concepts and authentic contexts that school communities choose as worthy of understanding.

Differentiating success criteria

The HOT SOLO DCM uses SOLO-differentiated self assessment rubrics to help clarify the learning and assessment focus for teachers and students across learning intentions, three-level assessment tasks and the knowledge-producing process. Here we examine each of these areas in turn.

Self assessing SOLO learning verbs (learning intentions)

Each SOLO learning verb (*define, describe, sequence, classify, compare and contrast, explain, analyse, form an analogy, predict, generalise, predict* and *evaluate*) has an associated HOT SOLO map and a text-based or visual self assessment rubric with SOLO-coded success criteria. The SOLO-differentiated success criteria for each learning verb provide a level of clarity that makes the "where to next?" steps achievable and builds student interest.

On the following pages you will find templates of text-based self assessment rubrics for each SOLO learning verb, along with student exemplars, which are SOLO differentiated. For the visual form of these self assessment rubrics and a full description of HOT SOLO maps, see Book 1 in this series.

Sample: Book 1 HOT SOLO resources

HOT SOLO Classify map

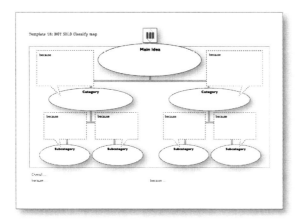

Visual self assessment rubric for HOT SOLO Classify map

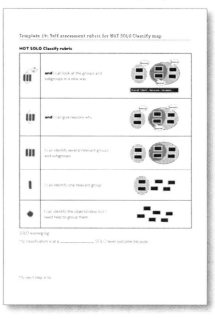

Template 2: Self assessment rubric for HOT SOLO Define map

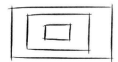

SOLO level	Success criteria	Student exemplar
	My definition statement identifies several relevant ideas; links these to the whole; **and looks at the linked ideas in a new way.** **"In a new way":** *generalise, predict, imagine, create, reflect, justify, evaluate, express a personal opinion* **Target vocabulary:** *overall, think, believe, it may, in the future, could include*	A barnacle is a living thing. The adult form lives "cemented" onto surfaces in marine environments; larvae are active swimmers in marine environments. It feeds on plankton by filtering plankton from seawater using modified feathery legs. Barnacles are at risk of drying out each day because they are exposed to the air and direct sun when the tide goes out. *Overall,* barnacles are well adapted for living in the intertidal zone because … because …
	My definition statement identifies several relevant ideas **and links these to the whole.** **"Links to the whole":** *sequence, classify, compare, make a causal explanation, make a part–whole analysis, form an analogy* **Target vocabulary:** *first, next, then, after, now, before, because, like, unlike*	A barnacle is a living thing. The *adult form* lives "cemented" onto surfaces in marine environments; *larval forms* are active swimmers in marine environments. It feeds on plankton *by* filtering plankton from seawater using modified feathery legs. Barnacles are at risk of drying out each day *because* they are exposed to the air and direct sun when the tide goes out.
	My definition statement **identifies several relevant ideas.** **Target vocabulary:** *and*	A barnacle is a living thing. It lives "cemented" onto surfaces in marine environments. It feeds on plankton. Barnacles are at risk of drying out each day.
	My definition statement **identifies one relevant idea.** **Target vocabulary:** *is*	A barnacle *is* a living thing.
	I need help to identify the idea to be defined.	I am not sure, is a barnacle something you find in the bath?

Template 3: Self assessment rubric for HOT SOLO Describe map

SOLO level	Success criteria	Student exemplar
	My description identifies the idea to be described; identifies several relevant adjectives or adjectival phrases; links these to convey an impression of the word; **and looks at the linked ideas in a new way.** "In a new way": *generalise, predict, imagine, create, reflect, justify, evaluate, express a personal opinion* **Target vocabulary:** *overall, think, believe, it may, in the future, could include*	The barnacle lives in a harsh and changeable habitat on the rocky shore. It is harsh because every day the habitat is exposed to the air and then covered by the sea. These environment changes mean the barnacle is at risk of drying out or washing off the rocks and can only feed when the sea covers the rocks. *Overall,* the barnacle's habitat will only suit a living thing with adaptations for living both in the sea and on the land.
	My description identifies the idea to be described; includes several relevant adjectives or adjectival phrases; **and links these** to convey an impression of the word. "Links to the whole": *sequence, classify, compare, explain the cause, make a part–whole analysis or an analogy* **Target vocabulary:** *because*	The barnacle lives in a harsh and changeable habitat on the rocky shore. This is harsh *because* every day the habitat is exposed to the air and then covered by the sea. These environment changes mean the barnacle is at risk of drying out or washing off the rocks and can only feed when the sea covers the rocks.
	My description identifies the idea to be described; **and includes several relevant adjectives** or adjectival phrases to convey an impression of the word.	The barnacle lives in a harsh and changeable habitat on the rocky shore.
	My description identifies the idea to be described; **and includes one relevant attribute**, adjective or adjectival phrase to convey an impression of the word.	The barnacle lives on the rocky shore.
	I need help to form a description.	I do not know where a barnacle lives (habitat).

Template 4: Self assessment rubric for HOT SOLO Sequence map

SOLO level	Success criteria	Student exemplar
	My statement identifies the idea to be sequenced, the relevant stages and the order of the stages; explains the order of the stages; and includes a generalisation or prediction about the sequence. **Target vocabulary:** *overall, think, believe, it may, in the future, could include*	The rocky shore food chain starts with phytoplankton (tiny floating algae) because they are autotrophs and use light from the sun to make food. Second in the chain are the zooplankton (tiny floating animals) which eat phytoplankton because zooplankton are heterotrophs and gain food from other organisms. Next come the barnacles which eat the zooplankton. After this come the speckled whelks who eat the barnacles. Black-backed gulls eat the speckled whelks. *Overall,* every food chain starts with the autotrophs because they can make their own food.
	My statement identifies the idea to be sequenced, the relevant stages and the order of the stages; **and explains the order of the stages.** **Target vocabulary:** *because*	The rocky shore food chain starts with phytoplankton (tiny floating algae) *because* they are autotrophs and use light from the sun to make food. Second in the chain are the zooplankton (tiny floating animals) which eat phytoplankton because zooplankton are heterotrophs and gain food from other organisms. Next come the barnacles which eat the zooplankton. After this come the speckled whelks who eat the barnacles. Black-backed gulls eat the speckled whelks.
	My statement identifies the idea to be sequenced, the relevant stages and the order of the stages. **Target vocabulary:** *first, next, then, initially, before, after, when, finally, preceding and following, rank, list, sort, order, timeline, starts, finishes*	The rocky shore food chain starts with phytoplankton (tiny floating algae). Second in the chain are the zooplankton (tiny floating animals) which eat phytoplankton. *Next* come the barnacles that eat the zooplankton. *After* this come the speckled whelks who eat the barnacles. Black-backed gulls eat the speckled whelks.
	My statement identifies the idea to be sequenced and several stages/steps. **Target vocabulary:** *first, second, next, last, finally, starts*	The rocky shore food chain *starts* with phytoplankton (tiny floating algae).
	I need help to sequence.	I need help to sequence a grazing food chain for the rocky shore organisms.

Template 5: Self assessment rubric for HOT SOLO Classify map

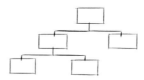

SOLO level	Success criteria	Student exemplar
	My classification identifies the idea/object to be classified and several related categories and subcategories; explains why the categories are linked to the whole; **and looks at the linked categories in a new way.** **"In a new way":** *generalise, predict, imagine, create, reflect, justify, evaluate, express a personal opinion* **Target vocabulary:** *overall, think, believe, it may, in the future, could include*	The starfish and sea urchin make a subgroup of the animals that live on the rocky shore because they all have tube feet. The crabs, hermit crabs and shrimps are another group because they all have a hard shell and jointed legs. A third group is the mussels, whelks and top shells because they all have shells made of calcium and a soft, slimy body. I could reclassify these rocky shore living things on the basis of their feeding behaviours – they are all heterotrophs but they get their food in different ways …
	My classification identifies the idea/object to be classified and several related categories or subcategories; **and explains why the categories are linked to the whole.** **"Explains why":** *give reasons, make a causal explanation* **Target vocabulary:** *because*	The starfish and sea urchin make a subgroup of the animals that live on the rocky shore *because* they all have tube feet. The crabs, hermit crabs and shrimps are another group *because* they all have a hard shell and jointed legs. A third group is the mussels, whelks and top shells *because* they all have shells made of calcium and a soft slimy, body.
	My classification identifies the idea/object to be classified, **and several related categories or subcategories.** **Target vocabulary:** *to group, to divide, to categorise, types, categories, groups, classes, kinds, examples, species, components, another*	The starfish and sea urchin make a subgroup of the animals that live on the rocky shore. The crabs, hermit crabs and shrimps are *another group.* A third *group* is the mussels, whelks and top shells.
	My classification identifies the idea/object to be classified **and related categories.** **Target vocabulary:** *group, subgroup*	The starfish and sea urchin make a *subgroup* of the animals that live on the rocky shore.
	I need help to classify.	They are all organisms that live on the rocky shore.

Template 6: Self assessment rubric for HOT SOLO Compare and Contrast map

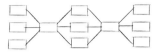

SOLO level	Success criteria	Student exemplar
	My comparison contains several relevant similarities and differences; explains why they are relevant; **and makes a generalisation.** **Target vocabulary:** *overall, think, believe, it may, in the future, could include*	A heterotroph and an autotroph are similar – they both need organic matter to stay alive and they are both organisms (living things). However, a heterotroph gets its organic matter from other living things because it cannot convert carbon dioxide and water into sugar and oxygen (photosynthesis) and an autotroph does not need to feed on other living things because it makes its own organic matter by the process of photosynthesis. *Overall*, the ability of an autotroph to manufacture its own organic matter rather than relying on other living things for food means the two types of living thing are more different than they are alike.
	My comparison contains several relevant similarities and differences; and **explains why** they are relevant to the whole. **"Explains why":** *gives reasons, explains cause* **Target vocabulary:** *because*	A heterotroph and an autotroph are similar – they both need organic matter to stay alive and they are both organisms (living things). However, a heterotroph gets its organic matter from other living things *because* it cannot convert carbon dioxide and water into sugar and oxygen (photosynthesis) and an autotroph does not need to feed on other living things *because* it makes its own organic matter by the process of photosynthesis.
	My comparison identifies **several relevant** similarities **and** differences. **Target vocabulary – compare:** *also, as, as well as, both, in the same manner, in the same way, like, likewise, most important, same, similar, similarly, the same as, too, still, in comparison, at the same time* **Target vocabulary – contrast:** *although, but, differ, even though, however, in contrast, instead, nevertheless, on the contrary, on the other hand, unless, unlike, while, yet, conversely, nonetheless*	A heterotroph and an autotroph are *similar* – they *both* need organic matter to stay alive and they are *both* organisms (living things). *However*, a heterotroph gets its organic matter from other living things and an autotroph makes its own organic matter.
	My comparison identifies **one relevant** similarity or difference.	A heterotroph and an autotroph are similar – they both need organic matter to stay alive.
	I need help to form a comparison.	I am not sure how to compare a heterotroph and an autotroph.

Template 7: Self assessment rubric for HOT SOLO Causal explanation map

SOLO level	Success criteria	Student exemplar
	My causal explanation identifies the event and several relevant causes and effects; explains or gives reasons why something is a cause or an effect; **and looks at the event in a new way.** **"In a new way":** *generalise, predict, imagine, create, reflect, justify, evaluate, express a personal opinion* **Target vocabulary:** *overall, think, believe, it may, in the future, could include*	Living on the rocky shore is hazardous because when the tide goes out organisms can dry out and/or overheat as a result of temperatures getting much higher in air than in water. Organisms stop feeding or reproducing because they seal themselves into their shells or find shelter to avoid drying out. Organisms are eaten by seabirds because they are exposed or they are washed off the rocks when the tide comes in again as a result of the force of the wave action. *Overall,* the factors making life hazardous are related to the rise and fall in sea levels *because ... because ...*
	My causal explanation identifies the event and several relevant causes and effects; **and explains or gives reasons why something is a cause or an effect.** **"Explains why":** *give reasons, give a causal explanation* **Target vocabulary:** *as a result of, because*	Living on the rocky shore is hazardous *because* when the tide goes out organisms can dry out and/or overheat *as a result of* temperatures getting much higher in air than in water. Organisms stop feeding or reproducing *because* they seal themselves into their shells or find shelter to avoid drying out. Organisms are eaten by seabirds *because* they are exposed or they are washed off the rocks when the tide comes in again *as a result of* the force of the wave action.
	My causal explanation identifies the event and **several relevant causes and effects.** **Target vocabulary – cause and effect:** *because, so, consequently, therefore, due to, since, as a result of, the reason for, thus, nevertheless, so that, if ... then, for, for this reason, this is how, accordingly*	Living on the rocky shore is hazardous *because* when the tide goes out organisms can dry out, overheat, stop feeding or reproducing, be eaten by seabirds or be washed off the rocks when the tide comes in again.
	My causal explanation identifies the event and **a relevant cause or effect.** **Target vocabulary:** *because*	Living on the rocky shore is hazardous when the tide goes out *because* organisms can dry out.
	I need help to make a causal explanation.	I need help to explain why living on the rocky shore is hazardous.

SOLO level	Success criteria	Student exemplar
	My part–whole analysis identifies the idea/object and several parts of the whole; and explains the effect of removing these parts. **It makes a generalisation about the function of the parts to the whole and evaluates the relative contribution of the parts to the whole.** **"Makes a generalisation … and evaluates":** *generalise, evaluate* **Target vocabulary:** *overall, I think, I believe, it may, in the future, the largest contribution*	The crab has four pairs of walking legs and one pair of claws. Without the claws, it would not be able to threaten attackers, carry food or dig itself into the sediment. *The claws' functions* are communication, defence and feeding. The claws are not necessarily *the most important part* of a crab because crabs without pincers anchor food with their walking legs and tear off bits to eat with their mouthparts. *[Repeat with the other parts.]*
	My part–whole analysis identifies the idea/object and several parts of the whole, **and explains the effect of** removing these parts (causal explanation). **"Explains":** give reasons, give a causal explanation **Target vocabulary:** *because*	The crab has four pairs of walking legs and one pair of claws. *Without the claws*, it would not be able to threaten attackers, carry food or dig itself into the sediment. *[Repeat with the other parts.]*
	My part–whole analysis identifies the idea/object **and several parts of the whole**.	The crab has four pairs of walking legs, one pair of claws, a carapace, stalked eyes, mouthparts and an abdomen.
	My part–whole analysis identifies the idea/object and one part of the whole.	The crab has four pairs of walking legs.
	I need help to analyse an idea/object.	I need help to analyse the parts of a crab.

Template 9: Self assessment rubric for HOT SOLO Analogy map

SOLO level	Success criteria	Student exemplar
	My analogy identifies the initial ideas involved (A and B) and the related attributes (a and b). It identifies the relational factor and forms a generalisation.	Watching the takeover of company X was like watching a black-backed gull take on a rock crab. Resistance was futile and after the act, there was little evidence of the original target apart from the odd fragments of claw.
	My analogy identifies the initial ideas involved (A and B) and the related attributes (a and b). It identifies the relational factor.	A rock crab may attempt to resist the black-backed gull but is swallowed completely – a target company may resist a takeover but the acquisition is carried out regardless. The relational factor is the futility of the resistance.
	My analogy identifies the initial ideas involved (A and B) and the related attributes (a and b). (For example, a is to A as b is to B.)	A rock crab may attempt to resist the black-backed gull but is swallowed whole – a target company may resist a takeover but the acquisition is carried out regardless.
	My analogy identifies the initial ideas involved (A and B). (For example, A is B.)	A black-backed gull eating a rock crab is a hostile takeover.
	I need help to form an analogy.	I need help to form an analogy between a seagull and a business practice.

Template 10: Self assessment rubric for HOT SOLO Generalise map

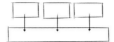

SOLO level	Success criteria	Student exemplar
	My generalisation makes a relevant claim; elaborates on it; and provides supporting evidence of the reliability **and the validity of the sample supporting the generalisation.** **Target vocabulary:** *overall, think, believe, it may, in the future, could include, expert opinion, considered plausible, independent research supports*	Rock pools (tidal pools) provide very different environments (for living things) when the tide is out. This is because when the tide goes out, the water in the pool is cut off from the sea. *Our environmental data show* that, without fresh supplies of seawater, the oxygen supplies in the pool water drop, and the temperature and salinity of the water in the pool increase. *Research shows* these factors have significant effects on the metabolism of living things.
	My generalisation makes a relevant claim; elaborates on it; and provides **supporting evidence on the reliability of the sample supporting the generalisation.** **Target vocabulary:** *overall, think, believe, it may, in the future, could include, the majority, many people, common knowledge, anecdote, personal opinion*	Rock pools (tidal pools) provide very different environments (for living things) when the tide is out. This is because whenever the tide goes out the water in the pool is cut off from the sea.
	My generalisation makes a relevant claim; and elaborates on it or clarifies terms. **Target vocabulary:** *by [x] I mean …*	Rock pools (tidal pools) provide very different environments (for living things) when the tide is out (low tide).
	My generalisation makes a relevant claim.	Rock pools provide very different environments when the tide is out.
	I need help to form a generalisation.	I need help to make a claim about rock pools.

Template 11: Self assessment rubric for HOT SOLO Predict map

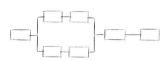

SOLO level	Success criteria	Student exemplar
	My prediction identifies a possible outcome; supports it with evidence in support of that outcome; and provides evidence that might negate the predicted outcome. I give reasons or explain why this evidence supports or negates the predicted outcome; **and make a generalisation judging the strength of the prediction.** **Target vocabulary:** *overall, think, believe, it may, in the future, could include*	I predict that I will be able to observe aggressive gull behaviour if I throw bread out at the rocky shore. This is because the bread will attract many gulls and the gulls will use aggressive behaviours to compete for food. They behave in this way around open rubbish bins in the city. However, if the gulls are not hungry, not enough may come. I have seen gulls ignore food when there is too much available so I may not see the aggressive behaviours. *Overall, I think* my prediction is strong because there is not a lot of excess food lying around the rocky shore like there is in a rubbish dump.
	My prediction identifies a possible outcome; supports it with evidence in support of that outcome; and provides evidence that might negate the predicted outcome. **I give reasons or explain why this evidence supports or negates the predicted outcome.** **Target vocabulary:** *because*	I predict that I will be able to observe aggressive gull behaviour if I throw bread out at the rocky shore. This is *because* the bread will attract many gulls and the gulls will use aggressive behaviours to compete for food. They behave in this way around open rubbish bins in the city. However, if the gulls are not hungry, not enough may come. I have seen gulls ignore food when there is too much available so I may not see the aggressive behaviours.
	My prediction identifies a possible outcome; **and gives evidence** (possible and actual) in support of the outcome and evidence (possible and actual) that might negate the predicted outcome. **Target vocabulary:** *however*	I predict that I will be able to observe aggressive gull behaviour if I throw bread out at the rocky shore. This is because the bread will attract many gulls. This happens around open rubbish bins in the city. *However,* if the gulls are not hungry, not enough may come. I have seen gulls ignore food when there is too much available.
	My prediction identifies a possible outcome and supports it with evidence (possible and actual) in support of the predicted outcome. **Target vocabulary:** *because*	I predict that I will be able to observe aggressive gull behaviour if I throw bread out at the rocky shore. This is *because* the bread will attract many gulls and they will fight over the food. I have seen this happen around open rubbish bins in the city.
	I need help to predict the outcome.	I need help to predict how I can observe aggressive gull behaviour.

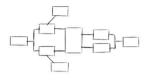

SOLO level	Success criteria	Student exemplar
	My evaluation gives reasons for the argument and explains why these reasons support it (helping premise); AND gives objections to the argument and explains why these objections work against it (helping premise). **It checks the reliability and validity of facts in the reasons and objections. It judges the reasons and objections individually and collectively and forms a generalisation.** **Target vocabulary:** *overall, think, believe, it may, in the future, could include, on balance*	*I think* our class should clean up the local beach because it has a lot of rubbish on it which harms the rocky shore organisms. The evidence for this is … Another reason is that no one else is cleaning it so we need to set an example to encourage others to help. The evidence for this is … However, some people object; they think it will be dangerous to collect the rubbish and that children should not get involved in activity where they might get cut or catch diseases. The evidence for this is … *Overall, I think* we should clean up the beach – the reasons for cleaning up the beach are convincing and the objections can be answered with the right safety measures.
	My evaluation gives reasons for the argument and explains why these reasons support it (helping premise); AND gives objections to the argument **and explains why these objections work against it (helping premise).** **Target vocabulary:** *reason, however, because*	I think our class should clean up the local beach *because* it has a lot of rubbish on it which harms the rocky shore organisms. Another *reason* is that no one else is cleaning it so we need to set an example to encourage others to help. *However*, some people object; they think it will be dangerous to collect the rubbish and that children should not get involved in activity where they might get cut or catch diseases.
	My evaluation identifies the argument and **gives reasons for AND objections to the argument.** **Target vocabulary:** *reason, objection, however, because*	I think our class should clean up the local beach *because* it has a lot of rubbish on it. Another *reason* is that no one else is cleaning it. *However*, some people object; they think it will be dangerous to collect the rubbish.
	My evaluation identifies the argument and **gives reasons for OR objections to the argument.** **Target vocabulary:** *should, reason, objection, should not*	I think our class *should* clean up the local beach because it has a lot of rubbish on it.
	I need help to make an evaluation.	I need help to decide if our class should clean up a local beach.

Self assessing three-level tasks

Each learning goal (concept, achievement objective, achievement standard or driving question) is unpacked into three summative tasks differentiated across three levels of SOLO Taxonomy – multistructural, relational and extended abstract. All students attempt the three-level summative self assessments, which are designed to help them identify when they have met a learning goal (see Table 3 for some examples). With differentiated tasks, students can self assess the relative depth of their understanding of the learning goal. This process values the NZC principles of *high expectations, coherence* and *learning to learn*.

Table 3: Examples of three-level self assessments

 For the concept of change

1. **Define** change. [multistructural task]
2. **Explain** the cause or consequence of a change. [relational task]
3. **Predict** a change. [extended abstract task]

 For the achievement objective: Understand how time and change affect people's lives (Social Sciences, Level 2)

1. **Describe** a change in people's lives. [multistructural task]
2. **Sequence** the changes in people's lives over time. [relational task]
3. **Generalise** about a change in people's lives over time. [extended abstract task]

 For the achievement standard: Describe how cultures change (Social Studies 1.1)

1. **Describe** the change involved (include the groups and their points of view). [multistructural task]
2. **Explain** the processes that led to the change (include different points of view). [relational task]
3. **Evaluate** the importance of the change to the groups involved. [extended abstract task]

By differentiating the three-level self assessment tasks (and providing visual process mapping and differentiated success criteria for each), we help all students to experience success in learning and build their confidence.

With the SOLO-differentiated self assessment rubrics for each learning verb (*define, describe, sequence, classify, compare and contrast, explain, form an analogy, analyse, generalise, predict, evaluate*), students and teachers can co-construct more nuanced self assessment rubrics against the three-level self assessment tasks.

Having differentiated success criteria for the three-level self assessment tasks makes the learning goal visible to students before they start the learning experience, which in turn builds student interest and confidence. Table 4 presents an example of a co-constructed self assessment rubric for tasks at the three levels designed for the achievement standard Social Studies 1.1.

Self assessing the knowledge-producing process

Co-constructed SOLO-differentiated rubrics help teachers and students to identify who is able to work independently at different stages of the research or inquiry process. By default these rubrics also identify those students who will need support to think like an expert in the domain – that is, those who need help to formulate a question, locate relevant information and data, collate data, analyse and create new knowledge, and/or present new knowledge and understanding. Templates 13 to 18 are samples of self assessment rubrics for the research or inquiry process when students are producing knowledge.

Table 4: Self assessment rubric for the achievement standard Social Studies 1.1

Task by SOLO level	Success criteria by SOLO level				
	Prestructural	**Unistructural**	**Multistructural**	**Relational**	**Extended abstract**
Describe [the change] involved. (Include the groups and their points of view.)	I need help to describe [the change] involved.	I describe one relevant attribute of [the change].	I describe several relevant attributes of [the change].	I describe several relevant attributes of [the change]; and make links between them. **Link:** *sequence, classify, compare and contrast, explain, analyse*	I describe several relevant attributes of [the change]; explain why they are relevant; and look at my description in a new way. **New way:** *generalise, evaluate, predict, reflect*
Explain the processes that led to [the change]. (Include different points of view.)	I identify the processes that led to [the change] but I need help to explain them.	I explain one relevant process that led to [the change].	I explain several relevant processes that led to [the change].	I explain several relevant processes that led to [the change]; and make links between them. **Link:** *sequence, classify, compare and contrast, explain, analyse*	I explain several relevant processes that led to [the change]; make links between them; and look at my explanation in a new way. **New way:** *generalise, evaluate, predict, reflect*
Evaluate the importance of [the change] to the groups involved	I make a claim about the importance of the change to the groups involved but I need help to give a relevant reason or objection.	I make a claim about the importance of the change to the groups involved; and give one relevant reason or objection.	I make a claim about the importance of the change to the groups involved; and give several relevant reasons and objections.	I make a claim about the importance of the change to the groups involved; give several relevant reasons and objections; and explain why these are relevant to the claim. For example: This is a reason for the claim because ….	I make a claim about the importance of the change to the groups involved; give several relevant reasons and objections; explain why these are relevant to the claim; provide evidence to support my reasons and objections; judge overall support for reasons and objections; and make an overall evaluation of the claim.

Template 13: HOT SOLO student research rubric: Asking questions

Possible question frameworks	SOLO Taxonomy learning outcomes		
	Multistructural	**Relational**	**Extended abstract**
	aware use	**strategic use**	**reflective use**
Level I Open–closed; 5Ws and IH; six thinking hats; SOLO learning verbs	I use … to ask questions but I am not sure why or when to use it. I make mistakes.	I use … to ask questions and **I know why and when** to use it.	I use … to ask questions, I know why and when to use it and **I seek feedback** on how I could improve my questioning.
Level 2 Question matrix; SOLO learning verbs	I can use … to ask questions that **bring in** information relevant to the subject.	I can use … to ask questions that **make links between** information relevant to the subject.	I can use … to ask questions that **look in a new way** at the information relevant to the subject.
Level 3 and above Ignorance logs; category lists; SOLO learning verbs	I can describe the purpose of my questions.	I can describe the purpose of my questions **and explain how the questions can bring in or link relevant information or look at it in a new way.**	I can describe the purpose of my questions, explain how the questions bring in or link relevant information and look at it in a new way **and reflect on how well the questions achieve their purpose.**
	Questions that *bring in* information ask you to: complete, count, define, describe, identify, list, match, name, observe, recite, select, scan, label.	**Questions that *link* information ask you to:** compare, contrast, classify, sort, distinguish, explain (why), infer, sequence, analyse, synthesise, form analogies, reason.	**Questions that *look in a new way* ask you to:** evaluate, generalise, imagine, judge, predict, speculate, state if … then, apply a principle, hypothesise, forecast, idealise.

Template 14: HOT SOLO student research rubric: Planning

Possible planning frameworks	SOLO Taxonomy learning outcomes		
	Multistructural	**Relational**	**Extended abstract**
	aware use	**strategic use**	**reflective use**
Level 1 Teacher directed	I can plan where to get resources.	I can plan where to get resources that link to my inquiry context.	I can plan where to get resources that link to my inquiry context, and plan for new contexts that may arise in the future.
Level 2 Sequence chart **Level 3 and above** Gantt chart	I can set up and track my research tasks on a timeline in a sequence or Gantt chart – but I make mistakes.	I can set up and track my research tasks on a timeline in a sequence or Gantt chart, and explain any differences between predicted and actual outcomes.	I can set up and track my research tasks on a timeline in a sequence or Gantt chart, and explain any differences between my predicted and actual outcomes. I can make improvements to my future planning in response to my actual outcomes.

Template 15: HOT SOLO student research rubric: Self evaluation

Possible self evaluation frameworks	SOLO Taxonomy learning outcomes		
	Multistructural	**Relational**	**Extended abstract**
	aware use	**strategic use**	**reflective use**
Level 1 Working with a teacher	I can describe the stages of my learning process. *[What I did]*	I can describe and explain the stages of my learning process. *[What I did and why I did it]*	I can describe, explain, evaluate and reflect on the stages of my learning process. *[What I did, why I did it, how it went and what I would change next time]*
Level 2 Using learning outcomes in SOLO Taxonomy **Level 3 and above** Using learning outcomes in SOLO Taxonomy	I can identify my learning outcome at different stages of the learning process. *My learning outcome is ...*	I can identify my learning outcome and explain why my learning outcome is at this level – at different stages of the learning process. *My learning outcome is ... because ...*	I can identify my learning outcome and explain why my learning outcome is at this level. I can evaluate my learning outcome and use this to predict next steps – at different stages of the learning process. *My learning outcome is ... because ... My next step is to ... because ...*

Template 16: HOT SOLO student research rubric: Bringing in information

Possible frameworks for bringing in information	SOLO Taxonomy learning outcomes		
	Multistructural	Relational	Extended abstract
	aware use	strategic use	reflective use
Level 1 Working with a teacher **Level 2** Using appropriate key words **Level 3 and above** Using different sources (primary and secondary) and cross-checking	I can [XXX] to access information. *[XXX]: work with a teacher, use appropriate key words, use different sources and cross-check*	I can [XXX] to access reliable information relevant to my inquiry question. *[XXX]: work with a teacher, use appropriate key words, use different sources and cross-check*	I can [XXX] to access reliable and valid information relevant to my inquiry question. *[XXX]: work with a teacher, use appropriate key words, use different sources and cross-check*

Template 17: HOT SOLO student research rubric: Making connections

Possible frameworks for making connections	SOLO Taxonomy learning outcomes		
	Multistructural	Relational	Extended abstract
	aware use	strategic use	reflective use
Level 1 Working with a teacher **Level 2 and above** Using relational learning strategies and interventions – ICT tools and thinking *Including HOT SOLO relational maps and self assessment rubrics – sequence, classify, compare and contrast, explain causes, explain effects, analyse, form an analogy*	I can [XXX] to sort information. *[XXX]: work with a teacher, use relational learning strategies and interventions – ICT tools and thinking*	I can [XXX] to sort information relevant to my inquiry question. I know why and when to [XXX]. *[XXX]: work with a teacher, use relational learning strategies and interventions – ICT tools and thinking*	I can [XXX] to sort and reflect on information relevant to my inquiry question. I know why and when to [XXX] and seek feedback to improve my use. *[XXX]: work with a teacher, use relational learning strategies and interventions – ICT tools and thinking*

Template 18: HOT SOLO student research rubric: Looking at it in a new way

Possible frameworks for looking at it in a new way	SOLO Taxonomy learning outcomes		
	Multistructural	Relational	Extended abstract
	aware use	strategic use	reflective use
Level 1 Working with a teacher	I can create a report on my learning.	I can create a report on my learning in response to my inquiry question(s).	I can create a report on my learning in response to my inquiry question(s) and include a reflection on the next steps for learning.
Level 2 and above [insert appropriate presentation strategies]	I can share my learning in a presentation with an audience.	I can share my learning from my inquiry question(s) in a presentation that is appropriate for my audience.	I can share my learning from my inquiry question(s) in a presentation that is appropriate for my audience. I seek feedback on my presentation and modify it in response.
	I can do something in response to my new learning.	I can do something in response to my new learning and explain why it is a result of my new learning.	I can do something in response to my new learning and explain why it is a result of my new learning, and seek feedback from others to improve what I do.

Differentiating learning interventions

Once teachers and students identify the SOLO level of the learning intention, they can identify the learning experiences, and the effective strategies (thinking strategies and/or ICT tools) that target the learning intention or learning goal.

Differentiating thinking skills and strategies

When thinking skills and strategies are categorised by the SOLO learning outcome they support, students create a portable thinking toolbox based on differentiated learning outcomes.

The thinking toolbox strategies supporting relational learning outcomes target learning goals that link ideas (*sequence, classify, compare and contrast, explain, form an analogy, analyse, ask questions* and so on) and may contain any of the following effective strategies (Hook 2006):

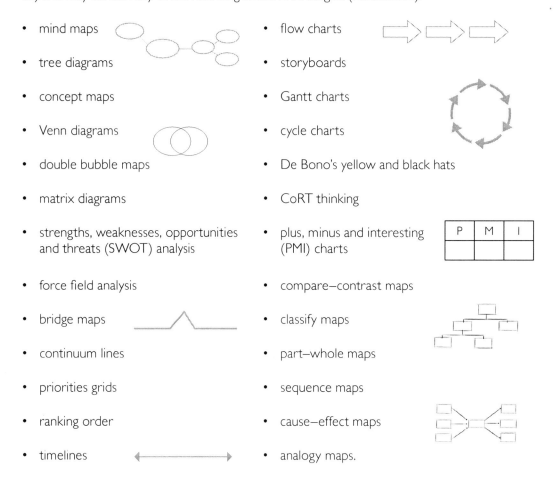

- mind maps
- tree diagrams
- concept maps
- Venn diagrams
- double bubble maps
- matrix diagrams
- strengths, weaknesses, opportunities and threats (SWOT) analysis
- force field analysis
- bridge maps
- continuum lines
- priorities grids
- ranking order
- timelines

- flow charts
- storyboards
- Gantt charts
- cycle charts
- De Bono's yellow and black hats
- CoRT thinking
- plus, minus and interesting (PMI) charts
- compare–contrast maps
- classify maps
- part–whole maps
- sequence maps
- cause–effect maps
- analogy maps.

For example, when attempting a learning experience designed to classify common materials (relational learning outcome), students can search the SOLO-coded toolbox for thinking strategies that offer graphical approaches to sorting and linking similar ideas within a hierarchical structure. To help clarify the links between categories or groups of similar common materials, students may choose to use a tree diagram, a mind map or even a concept map. When students can purposefully select effective thinking strategies to support an identified learning goal they build interest and confidence in learning.

Template 19 offers further examples of SOLO-differentiated thinking strategies that can be used in schools when planning with the HOT SOLO DCM.

Template 19: SOLO-differentiated thinking skills and strategies

Thinking skills intervention	Student learning outcomes coded by SOLO Taxonomy		
	Multistructural	**Relational**	**Extended abstract**
	SOLO Bringing in ideas: *identify, label, list, define, describe, retell, recall, recite*	**SOLO Linking ideas**: *compare, contrast, make a causal explanation, sequence, classify, make a part–whole analysis, explain, classify, question*	**SOLO Putting linked ideas in another context**: *predict, generalise, imagine, reflect, evaluate, create*
Hooked-on-Thinking SOLO maps and self assessment rubrics	Describe map Define map Identify map	Compare–contrast map Classify map Part–whole map Sequence map Cause–effect map Analogy map	Generalise map Evaluate map Predict map
De Bono's six thinking hats	White hat Red hat	Yellow hat Black hat	Blue hat Green hat
De Bono Cognitive Research Trust (CoRT) thinking programme and Direct Attention Thinking Tools (DATT)	CAF (consider all factors) KVI (key values involved)	PMI (plus, minus, interesting) RAD (recognise, analyse, divide) OPV (other people's view) FIP (first important priorities)	C&S (consequence and sequel) AGO (aims, goals, objectives) APC (alternatives, possibilities, choices) DOCA (decisions/design, outcome, channels, action)
Curriculum based reflections			Reflective journals/ Jeni Wilson triggers/ Mrs Potter's questions
Graphic organisers	Target maps Circle maps Single set diagrams Single bubble maps Splay diagrams Spider diagrams Webbing Concept maps Cluster maps Central idea graphs Brainstorm maps Explosion charts	Affinity diagrams Mind maps Tree diagrams Concept maps Vee maps Venn diagrams Double bubble maps Matrix diagrams Force field analysis SWOT analysis Bridge maps Continuum lines Priorities grids Ranking order Timelines Flow charts Cycle charts Storyboards Gantt charts	Fishbone diagrams Relations diagrams Critical path analysis Algorithms Systems diagrams Flowscapes Reason!Able argument maps Rationale bCisive

continued …

Thinking skills intervention	Multistructural Bringing in ideas	Relational Linking ideas	Extended abstract Putting linked ideas in another context
Question frameworks	Open–closed		
	Who/what/where/when	Why/how	
Tony Ryan's thinkers keys	The alphabet key The variations key The picture key The brainstorming key	The reverse listing key The disadvantages key The BAR key The alphabet key The variations key The picture key The commonality key The question key The brainstorming key	The what if key The combination key The prediction key The different uses key The ridiculous key The inventions key The brick wall key The construction key The forced relationships key The alternative key The interpretation key

Differentiating e-learning strategies and resources

It is also possible to align e-learning resources and ICT with different SOLO learning outcomes, allowing students and teachers to select e-learning strategies to more effectively target a learning goal.

Differentiating e-learning applications and approaches against SOLO outcomes changes the way teachers think about the way their students use ICT (Hook 2006). Teachers no longer focus on whether their students can understand how to use different ICT applications at different levels of the school.

For example, you may be accustomed to hearing teachers saying that at the end of Years 1 and 2 students will be able to use Kid Pix, Microsoft PowerPoint and VoiceThread. With the HOT SOLO DCM, however, teachers talk instead about ICT as learning interventions. They hold professional learning discussions on how well their students can use ICT to bring in ideas (SOLO multistructural learning outcomes). They plan relational learning experiences that explicitly require students to link ideas using ICT (SOLO relational learning outcomes). They take time to show students how to use ICT to look at linked ideas in a new way (SOLO extended abstract learning outcomes). So, for example, you are more likely to hear teachers stating that by the end of Years 1 and 2 students will be able to bring in information in two or three different ways using ICT.

When teachers and students differentiate ICT applications and strategies against SOLO outcomes they can self assess their use of e-learning strategies against a SOLO-differentiated rubric, such as the one set out in Table 5.

Table 5: ICT use aligned to an identified learning intention

Learning intention – for example ...	ICT use by SOLO level				
Multistructural learning intention Relational learning intention Extended abstract learning intention	I need help to use ICT aligned to an identified learning intention.	I use ICT aligned to an identified learning intention when I am directed to on the team's long-term plan.	I use a number of different ICT tools that are on my team's long-term plan but I am not sure why or when it is best to use them so I make mistakes.	I use ICT to support an identified learning intention and can explain why/how my ICT supports an identified learning intention in my planning.	I seek feedback and make judgements about which ICT use is most appropriate for meeting my learning intention.
Effective strategies	*[Insert strategies suggested by students and teachers.]*				

We can better understand the different approaches that teachers (and students) take to selecting ICT tools by using SOLO coding to interpret their decisions. Thus teachers (and students) who have a **unistructural** understanding of selecting ICT tools to support an identified learning intention will make decisions based on direction. They will say things like:

Our school uses Mathletics for maths.
I use the IWB like a whiteboard. For example, I can use the pen on the IWB to write.
I used Glogster because it was suggested at our team meeting.

Teachers (and students) who have a **multistructural** understanding of selecting ICT tools to support an identified learning intention will make decisions but will not be confident about the reasons behind their decisions. They will operate by trial and error. For example, they may say:

Our school uses Mathletics, Digistore and Rainforest Maths for maths.
I am aware I can use many tools on the IWB. For example, I can use the pen, ruler, rubber, internet and my content.
I am aware the tools you can use in Glogster, such as video, sound, image, text and graphics, will engage my class.

Teachers (and students) who have a **relational** understanding of selecting ICT tools to support an identified learning intention are purposeful. They know why and when to select an ICT tool. For example, they may say:

When we learn geometry, we use "triangle trouble" from Mathletics because we are learning to classify triangles.
I can say why I have chosen the tool I am using on the IWB and how it supports our learning intention. For example, I am using the protractor on the IWB because it is big, clear and moveable and I can make a video to continue the modelling while my students are working.
I am using Glogster with my students because it enables them to connect multi-literacy to show their understanding.

Teachers (and students) who have an **extended abstract** understanding of selecting ICT tools to support an identified learning intention seek feedback on how they could improve what they are doing. They will say things like:

I have chosen to use the protractor rather than BBC Skillwise because I can use my own examples.
I have chosen to use Glogster rather than PowerPoint because: a wider audience can view it; we can use it to develop home–school partnerships; it links between content on one page; it is easy to use, including for embedding; and students can continue to work on it from home.

When students purposefully select effective ICT resources, applications and strategies to support an identified learning goal, they build an interest and confidence in their learning. For example, when attempting a learning experience designed to sequence the development of common materials (a relational learning outcome), they can search their SOLO-coded ICT toolbox for approaches and resources that offer e-learning approaches to sequencing ideas. Students might choose an online mapping program to create a sequence map, mind map or even a concept map to help clarify the links between sequential ideas or events involved in the production of plastic, metal or glass. They might choose to collaborate with others to sequence the development of a common material on:

- xtimeline www.xtimeline.com
- timetoast www.timetoast.com
- Dipity www.dipity.com

To sequence the development students might choose to use Microsoft Photo Story or PowerPoint or Apple's Keynote. Alternatively they might escape the relentless sequentiality of such software by choosing from the options available within the zoomable canvas of:

- Prezi http://prezi.com

For ideas on building a SOLO-differentiated e-learning resource, see Template 20.

Template 20: SOLO-differentiated e-learning strategies and some suggested resources

Multistructural	Relational	Extended abstract
e-learning for bringing in ideas *identify, label, list, define, describe, retell, recall, recite*	**e-learning for linking ideas** *compare, contrast, make a causal explanation, sequence, classify, make a part–whole analysis, explain, classify, form an analogy*	**e-learning for putting linked ideas in another context** *predict, hypothesise, generalise, imagine, reflect, evaluate, create*
Define (What is ...?) Google Dictionary Definitions strategy www.google.com/help/features.html	**Cluster search engine** Yippy http://yippy.com	**Reflection** – blogs Google Blogger www.blogger.com
Search engine for students Quintura Kids (visual search engine for children) http://quinturakids.com	**Mapping tools** Visual Understanding Environment http://vue.tufts.edu	**Create and share – video** YouTube www.youtube.com
Web feed aggregator Google Reader www.google.com/reader	**Sequencing** xtimeline http://xtimeline.com	**Debate** Debategraph http://debategraph.org
ESOL resources Shahi Visual Online Dictionary http://blachan.com/shahi	**Comparison** ReadWriteThink comparison tool www.readwritethink.org and search for "compare and contrast map"	**Argument** Debatepedia http://debatepedia.idebate.org
Wikipedia Wikipedia Selection for Schools http://schools-wikipedia.org	**Classify** Galaxy Zoo www.galaxyzoo.org	**Discussion** Power League www.powerleague.org.uk
Images Flickr http://flickrcc.bluemountains.net	**Asking questions** SurveyMonkey www.surveymonkey.com	**Create and share – wiki** Wikispaces www.wikispaces.com
Maps National Geographic Education MapMaker 1 http://education.nationalgeographic.com/education/mapping/outline-map/?ar_a=1	**Concept mapping** MindMeister www.mindmeister.com	**Create – 3D images** Google SketchUp http://sketchup.google.com
Te Reo Māori Māori Dictionary www.maoridictionary.co.nz	**Compare stories** International Children's Digital Library http://en.childrenslibrary.org	**Create collaborative documents** Google Docs https://docs.google.com

Checking for relevance and authenticity

It is a challenging task to identify learning goals that are relevant to the needs of diverse students living in local communities in a rapidly changing world. It requires teachers and students to look for the concepts or big ideas that lie beneath the NZC achievement objectives and achievement standards and to seek key competencies, values, learning interventions and local national and global contexts that resonate with students' lives and with local community needs.

When relevant learning goals are identified, differentiated and integrated into responsive learning environments, and students experience success through effort and the use of effective strategies, then students build on their levels of achievement, interest and confidence in learning.

Using concepts and big ideas

Introducing concepts allows students to engage with universals – timeless, abstract ideas that helped develop enduring understandings of complex issues in the past, remain useful in the present and are likely to be worth understanding in the future. A future focus is important when preparing diverse students for living in a rapidly changing world.

When schools involve their students and wider school community – including family and whānau – in the selection of concepts, they help to keep students' learning relevant and authentic now and in the future. Examples include *universals* like language, communication, stories and play, and *concepts* like change, systems, form, function and pattern. The NZC *Treaty of Waitangi* principle of acquiring knowledge of te reo Māori me ona tikanga is addressed through the adoption of Māori world views like tūrangawaewae – a place to stand; whanaungatanga – relationships and connectedness; and manaakitanga – generosity of spirit and respect. Table 6 offers a list of macroconcepts and Māori worldviews; Table 7 lists microconcepts schools have used when planning using the HOT SOLO DCM.

Table 6: Macroconcepts and Māori world views for future focus

Macroconcepts	Te ao Māori
Form	Tūrangawaewae – a place to stand
Function	Whanaungatanga – relationships and connectedness
Systems	
Structure	Manaakitanga – generosity of spirit and respect
Change	Whakataukī – stories, proverbs and communication
Communities	
Order	Tino rangatiratanga – self-management and determination
Constancy	
Symbolism	Kaitiakitanga – guardianship
Relationships	Taonga – a treasured thing
Measurement	Ako – to learn, to study, to teach
Patterns	
Complexity	
Cycles	
Movement	
Perspective	

Table 7: Microconcepts for future focus

Abundance and scarcity	Equilibrium	Physical world
Acceptance and rejection	Equity and access	Place and space
Achievement	Evolution	Politics
Action and reaction	Exploration	Position
Adaptation	Fairness	Power
Ageing/maturity	Feelings	Production
Ako	Freedom from and freedom to	Proof
Angle	Friendship	Reliability
Authority	Future	Religion
Balance	Gender	Renewable
Behaviour	Globalisation	Repetition
Beliefs and values	Growth	Resources
Cause and effect	Harmony	Revolution
Change and continuity	Honour	Rhythm
Character	Human rights	Rite of passage
Citizenship	Identity	Rights and responsibilities
Communication	Imagination	Ritual
Conflict	Indigenous people	Rules and laws
Conflict and cooperation	Individuals and groups	Safety
Connectedness	Innocence	Similarity and difference
Connections	Institutions	Social organisation
Conservation	Interactions	Society
Consumption	Interdependence	Space
Control	Invention	Success
Cooperation and competition	Isolation	Supply and demand
Correlation	Justice	Survival
Courage	Kaitiakitanga	Taonga
Creativity	Language	Technology
Culture	Leisure and labour	Time
Customs and practices	Liberty	Timing
Cycles	Lifestyles	Tino rangatiratanga
Decision-making	Line	Tradition
Defence/protection	Living and non-living	Transformation
Democracy	Loyalty	Transition
Development	Mana	Tūrangawaewae
Direction	Metaphor	Tyranny
Discovery	Migration	Uncertainty
Distribution	Mood	Validity
Diversity	Needs and wants	Variance
Ecological sustainability	Niche	Wealth
Energy	Organisation	Wellbeing
Enterprise	Paradox	Whakataukī
Environment	Perception	

The chosen concepts (and contexts) are unpacked using "What is worth understanding?" type questions (Wiske 1998) to develop key concept understandings. These generalisations underpin the concept and help students understand their world now and in the future. For an exploration of concepts, see Table 8.

Table 8: Exploring concepts – some examples

	Concept			
	Change	**Responsibility**	**Place**	**Communication**
Enduring understanding	Change is the process of moving from one state to another.	Responsibility is choosing to do the right thing.	Place is a space that people have made connections to.	Communication needs one person to send a message and another person to receive and make meaning from the message.

Finding a context

While choosing a relevant concept, the school community focuses on local and community needs and interests, which become authentic contexts for learning and building knowledge around that concept. Providing authentic contexts for learning helps meet the NZC principles of *community engagement* (connecting students' learning experiences with wider lives and engaging the support of their families, whānau and communities) and *cultural diversity* (valuing the histories and traditions of all people).

These authentic contexts can align to cultural, community and/or disciplinary understanding. To find an authentic context for exploring "place", a school community might discuss different perspectives from individual to global, as Table 9 illustrates.

Contexts allow relevance by introducing many different perspectives. Students could explore "place" by describing past, present and future perspectives of a local, national or global place (how we got here and where we are going). For example, in relation to how we got to a specific place and where we are going, they might describe:

- a Māori world view
- a story
- a myth
- a tourist's view
- an astronomer's view
- a refugee's view
- a politician's view
- an economist's view
- a religious view
- a spiritual view
- an anthropologist's view
- a local artist's view
- a local student's view
- a medical doctor's view
- a genealogist's view
- a preschooler's view
- a local shopkeeper's view
- a cartographer's view
- a town planner's view
- a past view (from X years ago)
- a present view
- an aerial view
- a Google Earth view
- a jogger's view
- an Aucklander's view
- a sign writer's view
- a geologist's view
- a tour bus driver's view
- a bird's eye view
- a satellite view.

Once they had developed a Māori world view of their chosen topic on how we got here and where we are going, teachers and students could then unpack it against SOLO learning verbs (using constructive alignment) to scaffold the learning intentions set out in Table 10.

Table 9: Examples of relevant contexts for the macroconcept of "place" and its significance for people

	Contexts for "place"			
	Individual	Local	National	Global
Examples	My family home – where I belong Tūrangawaewae	Pūriri tree in school playground A local skateboard park A local river A local graveyard	The Beehive Tongariro National Park The Sky Tower Waitangi	The Amazon rainforest Panama Canal The Great Wall of China

Table 10: Using SOLO learning verbs to scaffold learning intentions for exploring a Māori world view

Define whakapapa. (What is it?)

Describe whakapapa. (What does it look like? sound like? feel like?)

Describe "te here tangata". (What does it look like? sound like? feel like?)

Retell a whakapapa.

Describe an ancestor who came before me.

Describe what they brought to this place (spiritual, educational, cultural, physical).

Describe who will come after me.

Describe what they will take with them.

Sequence the stages in [how we got here and where we are going].

Sequence the people/offspring in [how we got here and where we are going].

Sequence the stages in how something was brought to a place and where it will go next.

Classify ways of viewing [how we got here and where we are going].

Compare and contrast this Māori world view with another view or perspective.

Explain how this Māori world view is passed on between generations.

Explain what caused this Māori world view.

Explain the effect of having this Māori world view.

Explain how and why this Māori world view is changing.

Explain how this Māori world view is connected to other things.

Generalise about your responsibility in regard to this Māori world view.

Reflect on the significance of holding this Māori world view.

Create an action that represents your view about what is important when holding this Māori world view and that shares it with others.

Through this approach, students can develop the generalisations they have formed from the concepts in a variety of authentic contexts that align with many different learning areas in an integrated curriculum. The framework allows diverse students to contribute genuinely new cultural, community or disciplinary knowledge from their learning. This approach builds interest and confidence.

Developing "what if ..." questions

"What if" questions:

- explore other points of view, perspectives, differences, alternatives, controversies and disputes – they help students interrogate complexity and ambiguity
- introduce unexpected, disconcerting insights and whimsical ways of knowing, while still valuing the NZC principles of *high expectations, coherence* and *learning to learn*.

Teachers and students generate "what if" questions aligned to a concept or an identified achievement objective or achievement standard. They use them as discussion starters, where participants look for possible causes or possible consequences. These questions can become a teaching and learning resource for home–school partnerships and topics for a P4C community of inquiry.

Table 11 provides examples of some "what if" questions that might be used in a primary school investigation of water.

Integrating values and key competencies

The HOT SOLO DCM can also integrate two other aspects of the New Zealand Curriculum:

- The NZC values are "deeply held beliefs about what is important or desirable" (Ministry of Education 2007, p 10). This element identifies the values to be "encouraged, modelled, and explored" through the learning experiences developed in planning.
- The NZC key competencies are "capabilities for living and lifelong learning" (Ministry of Education 2007, p 12). This stage encourages their thoughtful integration in the authentic contexts and achievement objectives selected to explore the concept.

For authentic and relevant learning, teachers and/or students use the HOT SOLO DCM to expand the values and key competencies within the learning experiences. Each value and key competency has a SOLO-coded, SOLO-differentiated self assessment rubric. The tables that follow offer two examples of co-constructed SOLO functioning knowledge rubrics:

- Table 12 focuses on blog commenting – a context for the NZC key competency of *participating and contributing*.
- Table 13 focuses on using technology in a way that respects others – a context for the NZC value of *respect*.

When teachers co-construct functioning knowledge rubrics such as these with their students, they support the NZC principle of *learning to learn*.

Table 11: "What if" questions for an investigation of "water" at primary level

What if you could drink only the water you collected off your own roof?

What if only rich people could afford to buy clean water?

What if you had to collect your water from a pump at the end of the road?

What if we banned mixtures from supermarkets and you had to buy everything separately in the raw state?

What if everything was mixed and you had to do your own separating?

What if New Zealand ran out of filter paper?

What if water could only exist as a liquid?

What if we shared all the clean water in the world equally?

What if we rationed water and when you ran out you could not buy any more?

What if we couldn't drink tap water?

What if water cost as much as fizzy drink?

What if you had to drink your own urine? (Go to www.scientificamerican.com and search for "new menu item on space station".)

What if you had to wear a special suit to catch all your sweat so it could be filtered and reused?

What if we had to use icebergs for our drinking water supply?

What if we all had to go back to using septic tanks?

What if you had to filter your water before you drank it using a LifeStraw? (Go to www.scientificamerican.com and search for "water filtration system straw".)

What if Christchurch did not have the sandy soil (aquifer) on the Canterbury Plains to filter the city's water supply?

What if we stripped all the guttering off the buildings?

What if everyone had to collect his or her own salt from the sea?

What if dissolving did not work?

What if nothing could melt?

What if sugar did not dissolve in water?

What if water did not evaporate from the sea?

What if water evaporated at room temperature?

What if all the free water in the world was frozen?

What if we had nowhere to separate mixtures?

What if selling mixtures was forbidden?

What if you had to mix everything before you used it?

What if we could eat only raw food?

What if we had not discovered how to make fire?

What if rainwater never soaked into the earth?

What if polluted water contained lots of dissolved oxygen?

What if all the water in the world got warmer and held less dissolved oxygen?

What if rainwater never touched the ground so no ground minerals could dissolve into it?

What if the Ministry of Health did not set drinking water standards for New Zealand's water supply?

What if the average New Zealand household was only allowed half of the 2,000,000 litres of clean water it uses each year?

What if the wastewater treatment plant at Mangere broke down and the 300 million litres of wastewater a day could not be treated?

What if water did not evaporate from the earth's surface?

What if the sun heated the earth evenly all over?

What if we covered the surface of the Hauraki Gulf in cling film?

What if we caught all the rain before it reached the earth's surface?

Table 12: SOLO self assessment rubric for the key competency of participating and contributing in the context of "blog commenting"

	Success criteria by SOLO level				
Participating and contributing through **blog commenting** – engaging in conversation online	I need help to read and comment on a blog post. *For example, blog comment does not refer to the ideas in the original post and/or shows a lack of awareness of how comments might affect others.*	I can read and comment on a blog post if directed to do so. *For example, blog comment makes a general reference to the original post.*	I can read and comment on a blog post. *For example, blog comment includes specific reference to the ideas from the original post.*	I can read and comment on a blog post. My comment reflects my understanding of the blogger's viewpoint. *For example, blog comment links ideas from the original post.*	I can read and comment on a blog post. My comment reflects my understanding of the blogger's viewpoint and offers a new perspective. *For example, in blog comment linked ideas from the original post are taken into other contexts.*
Effective strategies	[Insert strategies suggested by students and teachers.]	Give feedback: "I agree with everything said so far."	Ask for clarification: "I'm just not sure what you mean by …"	Ask for explanation: "What do you think led to this?"	Ask for new thinking: "Do you think X is an alternative to this situation?"

44

Table 13: SOLO self assessment rubric for the value of respect in the context of "using technology in a way that respects others"

		Success criteria by SOLO level			
Respect: Using technology in a way that respects others	I need help to respect others' feelings and/or privacy when using technology. For example, "I do not know why he is upset about me sharing it – it was a funny photo."	I can use technology in a way that respects others' feelings and/or privacy if directed to do so. For example, "Okay if you insist, I will delete the video."	I can use technology in a way that respects others' feelings and/or privacy but I am not sure why or when I should do this so I make mistakes. For example, "It is probably okay – let's post it and see what happens."	I can use technology in a way that respects others' feelings and/or privacy. I know why and when to do this. For example, "I am waiting until I get permission from the people in the photos before I put them online."	I can use technology in a way that respects others' feelings and/or privacy. I know why and when to do this. I reflect on how I use technology and seek feedback on how to improve. For example, "Use this password to check out the video. If anyone is having second thoughts about giving permission, let me know and we can re-edit."
Effective strategies	[Insert strategies suggested by students and teachers.]		Is it hurtful? Would I say or do this in person?	Is it legal?	

Meeting the principles in the New Zealand Curriculum

The pedagogical design of the HOT SOLO DCM keeps a tight focus on the principles in the New Zealand Curriculum: "beliefs about what is important and desirable in school curriculum – nationally and locally" (Ministry of Education 2007, p 9). These links are made explicit in Table 14 below.

Table 14: HOT SOLO DCM design elements used to support the New Zealand Curriculum principles

Why do we have a curriculum? What is our purpose?	
"Young people who will be confident, connected, actively involved, lifelong learners." (Ministry of Education 2007, p 8)	
What are the NZC principles to inform this purpose?	
"Principles put students at the centre of teaching and learning, asserting that they should experience a curriculum that engages and challenges them, is forward-looking and inclusive, and affirms New Zealand's unique identity." (Ministry of Education 2007, p 9)	
Principle	**How does HOT SOLO DCM achieve this principle?**
Put the learner at the centre of teaching and learning Be responsive to the learner by respecting individual abilities and interests. The individual identifies their learning needs with support from the institution.	HOT SOLO DCM: • allows for flexible provision – the user determines content, process, product and learning environment, supported by the system • provides authentic contexts for learning • builds knowledge for local and community needs • differentiates learning experiences against student learning outcomes (SOLO constructive alignment).
Experience engagement when learning Become actively involved in designing and assessing their learning. Become assessment capable.	HOT SOLO DCM provides: • HOT SOLO-coded self assessment rubrics • a HOT SOLO-coded integrated planning template • knowledge building for local and community needs.
High expectations Achieve personal excellence. Experience challenge when learning.	HOT SOLO DCM: • recognises prior learning • integrates multilevel achievement objectives from NZC • constructively aligns learning intentions to achievement objectives • provides cognitively differentiated SOLO-coded learning experiences • includes three differentiated tasks (SOLO) for performance for understanding • provides HOT SOLO-coded self assessment rubrics.

continued …

Table 14: HOT SOLO DCM design elements used to support the New Zealand Curriculum principles (continued)

Principle	How does HOT SOLO DCM achieve this principle?
Treaty of Waitangi Acquire knowledge of te reo Māori me ona tikanga.	HOT SOLO DCM: • incorporates both macroconcepts and microconcepts of te ao Māori • aligns authentic contexts to concepts • differentiates learning experiences against student learning outcomes (SOLO constructive alignment).
Cultural diversity Value the histories and traditions of all its people.	HOT SOLO DCM: • includes a HOT Concept Library • provides authentic contexts for learning • builds knowledge for local and community needs.
Inclusion Address the learning needs of all students.	HOT SOLO DCM provides: • cognitively differentiated, SOLO-coded learning experiences • HOT SOLO-coded self assessment rubrics.
Learning to learn Be able to answer: • What am I doing? • How am I doing? • What do I do next?	HOT SOLO DCM: • provides a common understanding of the learning process based on differentiated learning outcomes (SOLO) and the NZC key competencies • aligns a common language of learning to differentiated learning outcomes (SOLO) • aligns common learning interventions (e-learning, ICT and thinking) to differentiated learning outcomes (SOLO) • aligns common classroom practice – including learning experiences, learning intentions and assessment for learning, as well as inquiry and problem-based learning – to differentiated learning outcomes (SOLO).
Community engagement Connect with wider lives. Engage the support of students' families, whānau and communities.	HOT SOLO DCM: • provides authentic contexts for learning • builds knowledge for local and community needs.

continued …

Table 14: HOT SOLO DCM design elements used to support the New Zealand Curriculum principles (continued)

Principle	How does HOT SOLO DCM achieve this principle?
Coherence Master disciplinary knowledge and skills across all learning areas in the NZC.	HOT SOLO DCM: • selects achievement objectives across learning areas and levels in the NZC • aligns learning intentions to achievement objectives • aligns learning intentions for the driving question • aligns three questions or tasks for understanding to differentiated learning outcomes • aligns learning experiences to differentiated learning outcomes • aligns learning interventions (e-learning, ICT and thinking) to differentiated learning experiences.
Future focus Prepare for living in a rapidly changing world. Understand complex issues.	HOT SOLO DCM: • identifies macroconcepts and microconcepts to explore universals • aligns authentic contexts to concepts • builds knowledge for local and community needs.

3. HOT SOLO DCM sample plan

The following plan (Table 15) may act as an exemplar for how the HOT SOLO DCM may be used with achievement objectives from the New Zealand Curriculum.

Table 15: HOT SOLO DCM sample plan

Concept: **Tūrangawaewae** ("a place to stand")		
Context	Values	Key competencies
Level One: Celebrations: Let's party at my place	**Excellence** Innovation	Thinking Managing self
Level Two: Marae: Another place, another way	**Diversity** Equity	Participating and contributing
Level Three: Migration: I am new in this place	**Community and participation**	**Relating to others** Making meaning from language, symbols and text
Level Four: Leadership: People shape places	Ecological sustainability **Integrity**	
Level Five: Land issues: Places matter to people	**Respect**	
Key understanding	Driving question	Subsidiary questions/tasks
My land, my people	How do I belong in this place?	1. *Define* place. (Multistructural outcome) 2. *Compare and contrast* an action or an event that impacts on our place. (NZ) (Relational outcome) 3. *Evaluate* the claim "People shape places and places shape people" (Extended abstract outcome)

continued ...

Table 15: HOT SOLO DCM sample plan (continued)

Curriculum learning area: *Social Sciences*

Unuhia te rito o te harakeke kei whea te kōmako e kō?

Whakatairangitia – rere ki uta, rere ki tai; ui mai koe ki ahau he aha te mea nui o te ao, māku e ki atu he tangata, he tangata, he tangata!

In the social sciences, students explore how societies work and how they themselves can participate and take action as critical, informed and responsible citizens.

Achievement objectives	Learning intentions
Level One (Celebrations: Let's party at my place)	
Understand how belonging to groups is important for people. Understand how the cultures of people in New Zealand are expressed in their daily lives.	*Define* groups, culture or celebration. List different groups or cultures in class *Describe* different celebrations. *Compare and contrast* different celebrations. *Sequence* a celebration. *Analyse* (part–whole) a celebration. *Classify* different celebrations.	*Explain* the importance of a celebration or why belonging to a group is important. *Predict* what would happen if people could not celebrate. *Create* a celebration for a person new to your class. *Generalise* about the importance of celebrations, the importance of belonging or the importance of place.
Level Two (Marae: Another place, another way)	
Understand how cultural practices reflect and express people's customs, traditions and values. Understand how the status of Māori as tāngata whenua is significant for communities in New Zealand.	*Define* Māori culture, tāngata whenua, culture, practices, traditions, protocol, or a marae or parts of a marae. *Describe* parts of the marae, a protocol at a marae, or a traditional Māori practice. *Compare and contrast* different marae or a traditional practice. *Sequence* a traditional practice at the marae. *Explain* the importance of a protocol at a marae.	*Analyse* (part–whole) the function of a marae. *Generalise* about the importance of customs for any culture. *Evaluate* why Māori culture is so important to New Zealand. *Predict* what would happen if we had no cultural identity. *Create* a protocol or practice for your home.

continued ...

Table 15: HOT SOLO DCM sample plan (continued)

Achievement objectives	Learning intentions	
Level Three (Migration: I am new in this place)		
Understand how the movement of people affects cultural diversity and interaction in New Zealand. Understand how early Polynesian and British migrations to New Zealand continue to have significance for tāngata whenua and communities.	Define migration, cultural diversity, cultural practices, traditions, Polynesian migration or British migration. List cultural diversity within your school or local area. Describe the drivers of migration, reasons for people migrating to New Zealand, the needs and wants of cultural groups in your area, Polynesian or British migration. Compare and contrast Polynesian migration and British migration; different aspects of cultures or of the journey of a migrant (eg, for a boat person and a business migrant). Sequence the journey of a migrant (past and present) or of a Polynesian traveller or a British immigrant. Explain why people chose to migrate to New Zealand; the significance of early migrations to New Zealand; or the impact of these migrations on your life as a New Zealander.	Classify the different reasons for migrating to New Zealand; the cultural diversity in your school, area or New Zealand; or the difficulties a new migrant faces. Formulate questions to ask a migrant. Analyse the positive impact of migration on New Zealand. Predict what would happen if the government stopped migrants from coming to New Zealand. Create a resource that could be used by new migrants arriving. Interview a migrant and create a migrant story to add to a digital archive that could be accessed by others or used as a resource for a new immigrant. Evaluate the statement that "migration benefits the country" or "the impact migration has on our area/country".
Level Four (Leadership: People shape places)		
Understand that the ways in which leadership of groups is acquired and exercised have consequences for communities and societies. Understand that events have causes and effects.	Define leaders, leadership or styles of leadership. List leaders or New Zealand leaders who have had a positive or negative impact. Describe the qualities of a leader or an example of leadership. Compare and contrast two different leaders; or the causes leading up to an event demonstrating leadership. Sequence the actions of a leader or the events that led up to a leadership decision. Analyse the qualities of leadership or the causes and effects that led up to an event.	Classify leadership styles. Explain the cause and effect of an event based on the decision of a leader. Formulate questions to ask a leader. Predict what would happen if all leaders had the same style of leadership. Evaluate the impact of a particular leader and the role they played in shaping an outcome in New Zealand. Make a generalisation about the need to have leaders in society. Create a toolkit as a resource for aspiring youth leaders.

continued ...

Table 15: HOT SOLO DCM sample plan (continued)

Achievement objectives	Learning intentions	
Level Five (Land issues: Places matter to people)		
Understand how the Treaty of Waitangi is responded to differently by people in different times and places.	Define the Treaty of Waitangi or the issues before or after the treaty or in the present day.	Explain the effect that the treaty has on our lives as New Zealanders today.
Understand how cultural interaction impacts on cultures and societies.	Describe an event before or after the treaty that impacted on life in New Zealand. List the people involved.	Analyse the roles of the people involved at the signing of the treaty or in issues in recent times; or the implications of the treaty for the people of New Zealand in recent times.
Understand how people's management of resources impacts on environmental and social sustainability.	Compare and contrast the needs of the Māori and the British; or the issues involved past and present.	Evaluate an issue of concern to New Zealand; or the statement that "All New Zealanders need to stand up and be counted".
Understand how the ideas and actions of people in the past have had a significant impact on people's lives.	Compare and contrast issues past with issues present; or two current treaty issues.	Generalise the importance of "place matters" in relation to the treaty.
	Sequence the development of treaty issues since the signing of the treaty.	
	Classify the issues that have arisen since the signing of the treaty.	

continued ...

Table 15: HOT SOLO DCM sample plan (continued)

Learning experiences that best meet the learning intentions and achievement objectives matching your students' abilities. Each learning verb in italics has an associated HOT SOLO map and written or visual rubric to support student learning outcomes.

Bringing in ideas identify, label, list, define, describe, retell, recall, recite	**Linking ideas** sequence, classify, compare and contrast, explain cause and effect, analyse part—whole, explain, form an analogy, ask a question	**Putting linked ideas in another context** predict, hypothesise, generalise, imagine, reflect, evaluate, create
Level One (Celebrations: Let's party at my place)		
Share a PowerPoint of images of a range of celebrations. Use a HOT SOLO *Define* map to *define* groups/cultures in class or celebrations, using pictures and text. List celebrations. Each day explore one (birthday, marriage, Christmas, mātāriki etc). Locate on a map the country in which each celebration originated. Use Google Earth (www.google.com/earth) to show each country relative to New Zealand. Share stories of celebrations or from other cultures. Invite guests to demonstrate an aspect of a celebration (dance, music, costume, food etc). List practices of a celebration. Use a HOT SOLO *Describe* map to *describe* a celebration or aspect of it. Use Wordle (www.wordle.net) to create a cluster of words around terms you *define*.	View photos or listen to an account of two similar festivals from a different cultural setting. Use a HOT SOLO *Compare and Contrast* map to state the similarities and differences. View two celebrations and using a *Compare and Contrast* map to explore the similarities and differences. Read about or view a procedure of a celebration (eg, food preparation, hāngi, dance) and represent it on a *sequence* map (http://xtimeline.com). Photograph part of a sequence to add to the *sequence* map. Build a class HOT SOLO *Classify* map using text, images and/or photographs of celebrations. Use VoiceThread (http://voicethread.com) to record students' explanations of different celebrations.	*Create* a celebration for a person or stuffed animal new to your class. Look at all of the aspects involved in other celebrations and select the elements you will include. Issue invitations (www.smilebox.com/invitations.html) and prepare (eg, dress) for the occasion. Use the HOT SOLO *Generalise* map to *generalise* about the importance of celebrations. Paste the generalisations onto a photo montage (www.photosynth.net). Students photograph their own celebrations that they attend and *create* a visual resource on celebrations that can be used for teaching purposes (www.photosynth.net).
Level Two (Marae: Another place, another way)		
Use a HOT SOLO *Define* map to *define* a marae using text and images (www.google.com/imghp). *Define* tangata whenua, tūrangawaewae, protocol, practices, kaumātua, pōwhiri, karanga, pepeha, whaikōrero, tapu, noa. *Describe* and sketch a practice or protocol. *Define* a meeting house (whare nui, whare tupuna), tekoteko, tukutuku, maihi, poupou, tāhuhu, kōruru, amo, Ranginui, Papatuanuku, Rongo-mā-tāne. *Describe* other places on a marae: whare kai, pātaka etc. *Define* one part of the meeting house, including a photo or image. Using a photo or image, *describe* this place. Invite a local kaumātua to describe a marae they knew while growing up. Locate this marae. Research iwi and marae (www.teara.govt.nz). Use Wordle (www.wordle.net) to create a cluster of words around terms you *define*.	*Compare and contrast* practices: at a marae and in daily life outside a marae; at urban and rural marae; at a marae in the past and a present-day marae (www.teara.govt.nz). *Sequence* a protocol or practice (eg, pōwhiri, hāngi, tangi) and explain each step. *Sequence* through photographs a visit to the marae supported with a written explanation of each step (www.timetoast.com). *Analyse* the parts of the marae, supported by images or photographs and stating the functions of each part. Using VoiceThread (www.voicethread.com) *explain* different protocols/practices and attach images.	*Create* an info graphic chart (an information visualisation picture: www.coolinfographics.com) that will inform visitors from another country about the correct protocols when visiting a marae. *Generalise* about the importance of customs for any culture. *Evaluate* why Māori culture is so important to New Zealand (www.wallwisher.com/build). *Predict*: what would happen if we had no connection to the past or to Māori culture. In groups *create* a protocol for your home, class or school. Practise it and follow it to welcome someone. *Create* a visual resource for another class preparing for a trip to a marae (https://prezi.com/desktop).

continued ...

Table 15: HOT SOLO DCM sample plan (continued)

Bringing in ideas *identify, label, list, define, describe, retell, recall, recite*	**Linking ideas** *sequence, classify, compare and contrast, explain cause and effect, analyse part–whole, explain, form an analogy, ask a question*	**Putting linked ideas in another context** *predict, hypothesise, generalise, imagine, reflect, evaluate, create*
Level Three (Migration: I am new in this place)		
Use a HOT SOLO *Define* map to *define* migration and reasons for it (economic, religious, political, social). List places that migrants in your class/school have come from, attach their photos in the relevant places on a world map and link to each place on Google Earth (www.google.com/earth). List the different reasons that migrants have come to New Zealand over time (eg, as explorers, goldminers, refugees: www.teara.govt.nz). Invite migrants to share their stories. Interview family and whānau for their stories. View migrant stories and images online (www.teara.govt.nz/browse). List the agencies that assist migrants on arrival. *Describe* the story of a migrant or migrant family, past and present. Make a wall display, including photos. Gather data from your local council on ethnic demographics in your area. List the needs and wants of migrant groups in an area. Walk around your area/city and list the influences that migrants have had. Visit your local supermarket and look at where the food comes from. Gather data on migration to New Zealand (www.stats.govt.nz/Census.aspx). *Define* Polynesian or British migration. *Describe* these journeys (www.teara.govt.nz). Use Wordle (www.wordle.net) to create a cluster of words around terms you *define*.	Set up a class wiki to share your own stories about where you or your family, whānau or ancestors originated. Gather data from your local council or the New Zealand Census and display them in an info graphic about the cultural diversity of your area or of New Zealand. *Formulate questions* for an online survey (www.surveymonkey.com) and invite people to answer them. *Explain* their journey to New Zealand. *Classify* the different reasons for migrating to New Zealand. *Classify* migrant stories under these headings. Include photos (www.photosynth.net). *Classify* positive and negative aspects of migration; the factors that help and hinder migration to New Zealand over time. *Compare and contrast* two migrant stories; Polynesian and British migration; a past and more recent journey. *Sequence* migration to New Zealand over time (xtimeline.com). *Sequence* the story of a migrant on a storyboard using Comic Life (www.comiclife.com). Write a report on the significance of migration to New Zealand.	*Create* an oral story after interviewing a migrant and create a podcast or video podcast (www.youtube.com/watch?v=-hrBbczS9I0 or search for "how to create a podcast" on YouTube). *Create* a resource that new migrants could use to help them settle into your community. Select a target age demographic and distribute the resource to the appropriate agencies. Interview a migrant and *create* a migrant story to add to a digital archive for others to access (www.photosynth.net, https://prezi.com/desktop). *Create* a chart telling the story of migration, past or present (www.chartle.net). *Evaluate* the statement that "immigration benefits the country" or that New Zealand should operate an open door policy. Present your evaluation as a debate.

continued …

54

Table 15: HOT SOLO DCM sample plan (continued)

Bringing in ideas *identify, label, list, define, describe, retell, recall, recite*	Linking ideas *sequence, classify, compare and contrast, explain cause and effect, analyse part–whole, explain, form an analogy, ask a question*	Putting linked ideas in another context *predict, hypothesise, generalise, imagine, reflect, evaluate, create*
Level Four (Leadership: People shape places)		
Define leaders and leadership. List New Zealand leaders (www.teara.govt.nz/en/biographies).	*Sequence* an event demonstrating leadership; a collaborative timeline of New Zealand leaders (http://xtimeline.com).	*Predict* what would happen if your leader had not been part of New Zealand's history. *Create* a class blog to present your outcomes. (For a tutorial, visit http://weblogs.about.com and search for "free blog at blogger.com".)
Define different styles of leadership (democratic, autocratic, laissez-faire).	Make a political cartoon *sequencing* an event involving your leader that made a difference to New Zealand (www.comiclife.com).	*Evaluate* what would happen if all leaders had the same style of leadership (democratic, autocratic or laissez-faire).
Describe the qualities of a leader.	*Classify* different styles of leadership; past and present leaders; qualities of a leader; or leadership causes and effects.	*Create* a class wiki to share and get feedback on your evaluation (www.wikispaces.com/content/for/teachers).
Describe an example of leadership. List leaders who have had a positive or negative impact worldwide or in New Zealand in particular.	*Explain* how your leader contributed significantly to New Zealand and present your explanation in a format of your choice.	*Evaluate* the impact of your leader on New Zealand society. Present your evaluation over a faded black-and-white image of your leader (www.photosynth.net).
Define causes and effects that have influenced leaders. List examples of causes and effects of leadership.	*Analyse* the qualities your leader has demonstrated and present your analysis as a report.	*Evaluate* the claim "people shape places and places shape people". Build a wall to share your evaluative statements (www.wallwisher.com/build).
Share stories or videos of worldwide leadership and specific areas of leadership – female, youth, academic disciplines, religious etc. Share stories of people who have influenced New Zealand society (www.teara.govt.nz).	*Formulate questions* you would ask your leader if you could meet them.	*Predict* what your leader's next speech would have been (or will be) about and *create* a podcast or video podcast of the speech as you predict it to share with others.
Invite a local or national leader (eg, in business) to explain their role and qualities. Make a photo gallery of New Zealand leaders (www.photosynth.net).	With a HOT SOLO *Cause and Effect* map, outline a decision your leader made. Place an image of your leader in the event box as well as outlining the event.	
Use Wordle (www.wordle.net) to create a cluster of words around terms you *define*.	*Compare and contrast* leadership styles; two New Zealand leaders; or world leaders.	
	Write an editorial that outlines and *explains* a decision your leader made and the issues that they face.	

continued …

Table 15: HOT SOLO DCM sample plan (continued)

Bringing in ideas *identify, label, list, define, describe, retell, recall, recite*	**Linking ideas** *sequence, classify, compare and contrast, explain cause and effect, analyse part–whole, explain, form an analogy, ask a question*	**Putting linked ideas in another context** *predict, hypothesise, generalise, imagine, reflect, evaluate, create*
Level Five (Land issues: Places matter to people)		
Define the Treaty of Waitangi, people involved, geographical area of iwi involved.	*Sequence* the key issues leading up to the protest or the events since the protest (http://xtimeline.com).	*Evaluate* the purpose of a particular protest and the outcomes. *Create* a class wall to collect and critique the work of others (www.wallwisher.com/build).
Define land issues, resources, environmental sustainability, land tenure, land occupation, Māori protest movement, political parties, tino rangatiratanga flag.	*Compare and contrast* two different land issues; past and more recent issues.	*Generalise* about the right to protest as a basic right. *Create* a static image to portray your message.
List issues that have arisen in New Zealand related to the treaty (eg, foreshore, river and lake access, forestry, drilling and mining, geothermal, off shore, land issues).	On a protestor's placard *explain* the outcome of these issues or of the protest (http://voicethread.com).	*Create* an info graphic or another kind of visual presentation to show the outcome of a protest over past or present land issues (www.coolinfographics.com, https://prezi.com/desktop).
View video footage or newspaper articles of protests such as Bastion Point, Raglan, Taipa, Whanganui Gardens, 1975 Land March and pastoral occupation (http://paperspast.natlib.govt.nz).	*Classify* the different issues related to this protest.	*Create* a PMI chart about the right to protest about "places that matter".
Identify leaders and *describe* their actions. *Describe* the key leaders, stakeholders involved, the issues involved and actions taken (www.teara.govt.nz/en/biographies).	Collect opposing viewpoints from a range of stakeholders and *analyse* your findings. Present your analysis as a plus, minus and interesting (PMI) chart.	*Predict* how the treaty will continue to impact on the lives of New Zealanders. Present your prediction in any format.
Define the key people and parties involved.	*Formulate* questions and use them to conduct a survey (www.surveymonkey.com). Graph the results to show how the public perceives or supports various treaty issues.	In a group, *evaluate* the claim "people shape places and places shape people". Present this evaluation to the class as a debate.
Use Wordle (www.wordle.net) to create a cluster of words around terms you *define*.	Collect newspaper articles supporting a range of viewpoints and *analyse* the information to show your understanding of the issue (http://paperspast.natlib.govt.nz).	
	If you could select only one treaty issue to support, which one would it be and why? *Explain* your answer.	
	Select a treaty issue. If you were prime minister of New Zealand, how would you respond to the protestors' claims? *Explain* your answer (http://voicethread.com).	

e-learning interventions to enhance conditions for …

bringing in ideas	**linking ideas**	**putting linked ideas in another context**
Google Earth (www.google.com/earth)	YouTube (www.youtube.com)	Prezi Desktop (https://prezi.com/desktop)
Microsoft Photosynth (www.photosynth.net)	TeacherTube (www.teachertube.com)	Wall Builder (www.wallwisher.com/build)
Māori Dictionary www.maoridictionary.co.nz	Google Images (www.google.com/imghp)	Microsoft Photosynth (www.photosynth.net)
National Library of New Zealand Papers Past http://paperspast.natlib.govt.nz	Comic Life (www.comiclife.com)	Chartle (www.chartle.net)
National Library of New Zealand (www.flickr.com/photos/nationallibrarynz)	timetoast (www.timetoast.com)	Audacity (http://audacity.sourceforge.net)
Wordle (www.wordle.net)	SurveyMonkey (www.surveymonkey.com)	Wikispaces for Educators (www.wikispaces.com/content/for/teachers)
	VoiceThread (http://voicethread.com)	"Tutorial: How to start a free blog at blogger.com" (http://weblogs.about.com and search for this title)

continued …

56

Table 15: HOT SOLO DCM sample plan (continued)

Self assessment rubrics for subsidiary questions and tasks

Teaching resources | "What if" questions | Integration

Multistructural learning outcome: Define belonging to this place.

SOLO level	Success criteria
Extended abstract	I can identify several relevant ideas about belonging to a place, explain these ideas and make a generalisation.
Relational	I can identify several relevant ideas about belonging to a place and explain these ideas.
Multistructural	I can identify several relevant ideas about belonging to a place.
Unistructural	I can identify one relevant idea about belonging to a place.
Prestructural	I need help to define belonging to a place.

Relational learning outcome: Compare and contrast an action or event that impacts on our place (New Zealand).

SOLO level	Success criteria
Extended abstract	My comparison contains several relevant similarities and differences about an action or an event, explains why they are relevant and **makes a generalisation** about how they impact on our place, New Zealand.
Relational	My comparison contains several relevant similarities and differences about an action or an event and **explains why** they are relevant to our place, New Zealand.
Multistructural	My comparison identifies **several relevant** similarities **and differences** about an action or an event that impacts on our place, New Zealand.
Unistructural	My comparison identifies **one relevant** similarity or difference about an action or an event that impacts on our place, New Zealand.
Prestructural	I need help to form a comparison.

Extended abstract learning outcome: Evaluate the claim "people shape places and places shape people".

SOLO level	Success criteria
Extended abstract	My evaluation gives reasons for the argument, explains why these reasons support it **and** gives objections to the argument and explains why these objections negate it. It checks the reliability and validity of facts stated in the reasons and objections. **It judges the reasons and objections individually and collectively and forms a generalisation** that "people shape places and places shape people".
Relational	My evaluation gives reasons for the argument, explains why these reasons support it and gives objections to the argument **and explains why these objections negate the argument. It checks the reliability and validity of facts in the reasons and objections for the argument** that "people shape places and places shape people".
Multistructural	My evaluation identifies the argument and **gives reasons for AND objections to the argument** that "people shape places and places shape people".
Unistructural	My evaluation identifies the argument and **gives reasons for OR objections to the argument** that "people shape places and places shape people".
Prestructural	I need help to make an evaluation.

Teaching resources	"What if" questions	Integration
Include any classroom and community resources that will support bringing in ideas, connecting ideas and putting ideas into another context.	Students make up five "what if" questions for use in class/group discussion or writing.	Suggestions for integration with other learning areas – science, The Arts, English.

Source: Curriculum information drawn from Ministry of Education. (2007). *The New Zealand Curriculum for English-medium Teaching and Learning in Years 1–13.* Wellington: Learning Media.

Note: For HOT SOLO maps, see Book 1 in this series.

4. Conclusions

To meet the needs of diverse students, the HOT SOLO DCM approach combines a heady mixture of SOLO Taxonomy, effective pedagogies, knowledge production and technology to enable diverse students to:

- learn how to learn
- be actively involved in designing and assessing their own learning
- experience appropriate cognitive challenge across all learning areas
- understand complex issues
- integrate ICT tools
- build knowledge about their local communities
- prepare for adulthood in a rapidly changing world.

The HOT SOLO DCM approach to planning is both responsive and comprehensive. Its elements have been designed to allow New Zealand schools to discover and develop student learning and knowledge production across local and community contexts in all learning areas and levels of the New Zealand Curriculum. This approach avoids simple solutions where technology is put forward "as some kind of magic fix" and it keeps a clear focus on the broader issues concerning pedagogy (Hook, in press).

Anecdotal reports suggest that learning outcomes are at a deeper level of abstraction when they result from the HOT SOLO DCM process. Students develop greater confidence with and interest in learning when they have freedom in and control over learning and can become producers of new knowledge that their community deems to be valuable. Further research is needed to understand in more depth the effect of this curriculum model on enhanced learning outcomes, student interest and student engagement. With the HOT SOLO DCM we need to look further again and observe the changes in how communities interact with schools when their students use this model to become knowledge producers and schools become knowledge resources for the local community.

5. Where to next?

The next step in the learning process with SOLO Taxonomy is to examine the capabilities for living and lifelong learning – key competencies and e-competencies, which we can use to live well and learn well in a rapidly changing world. The third book in this series explores how to use SOLO Taxonomy to meet the New Zealand Curriculum key competencies (thinking, relating to others, managing self, participating and contributing and using language symbols and texts) and the e-competencies (e-awareness, technological literacy, media literacy, digital literacy, informational literacy; see Cobo Romani 2009). The book provides templates and examples showing how to use SOLO Taxonomy and self assessment rubrics as effective strategies for learning.

References

Biggs, J., & Collis, K. (1982). *Evaluating the Quality of Learning: The SOLO Taxonomy.* New York: Academic Press.

Bigum, C. (2004). Rethinking schools and community: The knowledge producing school. *Using Community Informatics to Transform Regions* (pp. 52–66). Hershey, PA: Idea Group.

Cobo Romaní, C. (2009). Strategies to promote the development of e-competences in the next generation of professionals: European and international trends. *SKOPE Issues Paper Series.* Published at the ESRC Centre on Skills, Knowledge and Organisational Performance, Department of Education, Oxford University & the School of Social Sciences, Cardiff University. No. 13, September. Retrieved 27 November 2011 from http://e-competencies.org

Fraser, D. (2000). Curriculum integration: What it is and is not. *Set: Research Information for Teachers,* 3: 34–37.

Hook, P. (in press). Teaching & learning: Tales from the ampersand. In L. Rowan & C. Bigum (Eds), *Future Proofing Education: Transformative approaches to new technologies and student diversity in futures oriented classrooms.* Springer.

Hook, P. (2006). A thinking curriculum. *Curriculum Matters* 2: 81–104.

Hook, P., & Mills, J. (2011). *SOLO Taxonomy: A Guide for Schools. Book 1: A common language of learning.* Invercargill: Essential Resources Educational Publishers Limited.

Ministry of Education. (2000). *Gifted and Talented Students: Meeting their needs in New Zealand schools.* Wellington: Learning Media.

Ministry of Education. (2007). *The New Zealand Curriculum for English-medium Teaching and Learning in Years 1–13.* Wellington: Learning Media.

New Zealand Transport Agency. (2011). *Case Studies: Hawera Primary School – smart planning leads to a learning journey.* Retrieved 27 November 2011 from http://nzcurriculum.tki.org.nz/Curriculum-stories/Case-studies/NZTA-case-studies/Hawera

Riley, T., Bevan-Brown, J., Bicknell, B., Carrol-Lind, J. & Kearney, A. (2004). *The Extent, Nature and Effectiveness of Planned Approaches in New Zealand Schools for Providing for Gifted and Talented Students.* Report to the Ministry of Education, New Zealand.

Roberts, J.L., & Roberts, R.A. (2001). Writing units that remove the learning ceiling. In F.A.Karnes & S.M. Bean (Eds), *Methods and Materials for Teaching the Gifted* (pp. 213–252). Waco, TX: Prufrock Press.

Taylor, S. (2001). *Gifted and Talented Children: A planning guide.* Christchurch: User Friendly Resources.

Wiske, M.S. (1998). What is teaching for understanding? In M.S. Wiske (Ed), *Teaching for Understanding: Linking research with practice* (pp. 61–86). Jossey-Bass.

Index of tables and templates

Lightning Source UK Ltd.
Milton Keynes UK
UKOW010100110212

187103UK00001B/19/P